# DOES GOD'S EXISTENCE NEED PROOF?

# Does God's Existence Need Proof?

RICHARD MESSER

CLARENDON PRESS · OXFORD

1993

Oxford University Press, Walton Street, Oxford OX2 6DP

Oxford   New York   Toronto
Delhi   Bombay   Calcutta   Madras   Karachi
Kuala Lumpur   Singapore   Hong Kong   Tokyo
Nairobi   Dar es Salaam   Cape Town
Melbourne   Auckland   Madrid
and associated companies in
Berlin   Ibadan

Oxford is a trade mark of Oxford University Press

Published in the United States
by Oxford University Press Inc., New York

British Library Cataloguing in Publication Data
Data available

Library of Congress Cataloging in Publication Data
Does God's existence need proof? / Richard Messer.
Includes bibliographical references and index.
1. God—Proof.   2. God—Proof—History of doctrines.   3. Phillips,
D. Z.   (Dewi Zephaniah)   4. Swinburne, Richard.   I. Title.
BT102.M465   1993   231—dc20   92–45110
ISBN 0–19–826747–9

3 5 7 9 10 8 6 4 2

Typeset by Graphicraft Typesetters Ltd., Hong Kong
Printed in Great Britain
on acid-free paper by
Bookcraft (Bath) Ltd., Midsomer Norton, Avon

*To*
*my parents*

# ACKNOWLEDGEMENTS

I am very grateful to all those both within and without the academic community with whom I have had profitable and inspiring conversations during the course of my research, particularly Professors Rubem Alves, John Hick, D. Z. Phillips, and Richard Swinburne. I am also grateful to Professor Marco Olivetti for his invitation to a conference on the Ontological Argument, which helped me to form the latter half of Chapter 6.

Peter Broadis, Petra Forster, Julie Messer, and John Perry have provided invaluable assistance with the preparation of the manuscript; and the many librarians and administrators I have encountered have provided consistently useful and good-humoured replies to my enquiries.

Finally, I would like to thank Dr Rex Ambler, who has provided not only intellectual support and motivation, but also the equally inspiring qualities of patience and friendship.

# CONTENTS

# Introduction

Norman Malcolm, in his paper 'The Groundlessness of Belief',[1] expresses surprise that the Proofs of God's existence[2] are the centre of hundreds of courses in the philosophy of religion, particularly in England and America. Malcolm found this surprising because, when he wrote the article which I have referred to, almost every philosopher liable to have been teaching any of these courses was utterly convinced of the invalidity of the Proofs. Today the situation is slightly different, with thinkers of the stature of Richard Swinburne and Alvin Plantinga endorsing the Proofs' validity.

[1] Norman Malcolm, 'The Groundlessness of Belief', in Stuart C. Brown (ed.), *Reason and Religion* (London: Cornell University Press, 1977), 154 f.

[2] The Proofs of God's existence are traditionally fivefold. There are four *a posteriori* arguments designed to demonstrate the existence of God from humanly observable phenomena or from the totality of things. These are the Cosmological Argument, which infers from the existence of the world itself or from a phenomenon within it such as causality the existence of a being which explains the world's existence or which prevents the infinite regress of causes, and this being is God; the Teleological Argument, which infers a Designer or Orderer from the presence of design and order in the world; the Moral Argument, which infers God from morality, either as the cause and explanation of our consciences and moral lifestyles, or as the being who can perform the highest good (in Kant's philosophy); and the Religious Experience Argument, which offers the existence of God as the best explanation of the experiences of many people which have been believed to be of something beyond the natural order.

The other proof is the Ontological Argument, which is *a priori*. Very roughly, this is an attempt to move from the concept of God to the necessary instantiation of that concept, or from the suggestion that perfection entails existence and that therefore the perfect being (God) exists. It is true of all five arguments, but of the Ontological in particular, that there is a more significant diversity of interpretations of the meaning of each one than is generally recognized. This is an important point, and one that I shall spell out in greater detail in Ch. 6.

I shall call the Proofs of the existence of God simply 'the Proofs' throughout the book. I also assume a weak sense of 'proof', meaning any traditional kind of philosophical justification by rational means.

I began my book with a similar, but not identical, worry to that of Malcolm. While his surprise could have been abated by the writings of Swinburne and Plantinga, mine could not. For my surprise lay at a deeper level, arising from the lack of major Anglo-American thinkers who addressed in any depth the prior question of whether the project traditionally undertaken by advocates of the Proofs, namely the rational justification of the existence of God, was one that should be taking place at all. What implications did it have for one's understanding of God, and for what one considered to be the task of philosophy, if one thought that the Proofs were an appropriate task? Surely there were dissenters from the traditional view, who described a God and who did philosophy in a way that left no room for rational justification of God's existence? And what philosophical and theological implications should this carry for such dissenters?

My research into these questions resulted in the discovery of a relativity of attitudes towards the Proofs engendered by a relativity of attitudes towards central philosophical and theological issues. The diversity of views about what philosophy should be concerned with concealed a divergence of philosophical faiths, one school having faith in philosophy as rational justification,[3] the other having faith in philosophy as grammatical clarification.[4]

Similar faiths were apparent in divergent theological attitudes also. While one school found the task of defining God a comparatively straightforward affair, the other reviled the very propriety of defining God. While one school exhibited faith in the language of religion referring to an external reality, the other exhibited faith in religious language as a particular framework which worked by its own peculiar set of rules.

Clearly a discussion of such fundamental attitudes was necessary before any fruitful reflection upon the subsidiary issue of the appropriateness of the Proofs could occur; and equally clearly, owing to the extreme diversity of views on such fundamental topics as the meaning of God and the proper role of philosophy, a discussion of the possible relativity of such views was also

---

[3] The empiricist and rationalist tradition of philosophy of religion, exemplified today by Richard Swinburne.

[4] The Wittgensteinian school of philosophy of religion, exemplified today by D. Z. Phillips.

required. Each philosophical school possessed its own fundamental tenets, but, to go further than the conclusion that to one school the Proofs were appropriate and to the other they were not, a concentration upon the interface of and communication between the two schools had to be paramount.

In discussing the relativity of fundamental philosophical and theological presuppositions, and the interaction between the two conflicting philosophical schools, I still share Malcolm's concern over hundreds of courses dealing with the validity of the Proofs. However, I have come to feel no concern over the teaching of the Proofs themselves if the myriad of issues which pertain to them and which arise from them are allowed their significance. It is a task such as this which I hope that I have gone some way toward achieving in my book.

# 1

# God and Religious Language

Since Plato, and the Neoplatonic influence on early Christian belief, the dominant strand of Western philosophical thought has considered it entirely appropriate to try to prove that God exists. There have always been dissenters from such a view: for example, amongst the early Church Fathers Tertullian described the Greek philosophy influencing Christianity as the foolishness of this world. Clement of Alexandria held the contrary view, that philosophy was a gift from God to educate the pagan world for Christ and to deepen believers' understanding of their own faith. As Father Copleston concludes on Clement's attempts to unite Greek philosophy and Christian religion, 'in the end it was the attitude of Clement, not that of Tertullian, which triumphed'.[1]

None the less, there have still been many philosophers who have dissented from Clement's approach. In this chapter and the next I will consider the accounts of God, religious language, and the role of philosophy which underlie the attitudes to the appropriateness of the Proofs encapsulated by Clement and Tertullian. I will contrast two current thinkers in particular, a traditional philosopher of religion, Richard Swinburne, and a Wittgensteinian, D. Z. Phillips, while also trying to show that my comments here apply to much philosophical thinking of the past and therefore beyond the confines of the work of two thinkers.

Although Swinburne and Phillips are representatives of particular philosophical traditions, they each have provided original and stimulating thoughts of their own to make them especially worthy of consideration. Swinburne has taken the classical Proofs and several others assumed by philosophers in general to have been conclusively invalidated by Hume and Kant, and has

---

[1] F. C. Copleston, *History of Philosophy*, vol. xii (London: Burns Oates and Washbourne, 1950), 15.

reinterpreted them as cumulative inductive arguments using modern probability calculus. Phillips meanwhile has taken the insights of early followers of Wittgenstein and the inchoate thoughts of Wittgenstein himself, and has applied them widely to many areas of contention within philosophy of religion. He has also used literature more widely than previous philosophers, implicitly recognizing the importance of indirect communication.

The originality of these thinkers, then, reveals the value of a discussion of their own views of the Proofs, while the fact that they each stand in major philosophical traditions reveals that discussion of their assumptions will have implications for philosophy as a whole.

## 1. THE MEANING OF RELIGIOUS LANGUAGE

The difference between traditional philosophers of religion and those unhelpfully labelled Wittgensteinian fideists[2] is often referred to as that between cognitive and non-cognitive understandings of religious language. Richard Swinburne's first book in his classic trilogy on the philosophy of religion, *The Coherence of Theism*, is an explicit presentation of a cognitive understanding of the meaning of the God of theism.

In this section I will give an exposition of the cognitive theory of religious language outlined by Swinburne, followed by the Wittgensteinian alternative, indicating the historical support for each position. In Swinburne's proofs of God's existence, three principles are adduced as vital: those of simplicity, credulity, and testimony.[3] I argue that there are at least three more vital, tacit principles needed for the Proofs to be appropriate: the

---

[2] e.g. by Kai Nielsen, *An Introduction to the Philosophy of Religion* (London and Basingstoke: Macmillan Press, 1982). The label is unhelpful because the Wittgensteinians show marked differences from the paradigm of fideism associated with Karl Barth. The main differences are that while Barth begins with the specifically religious phenomenon of God, Wittgenstein begins with the universally shared phenomenon of language and practice; and while Barth is widely seen to dissociate religious language from other forms of language, Wittgenstein does not do so. (This is contrary to what is usually supposed, and I shall defend my position fully in ch. 3.)

[3] Richard Swinburne, *The Evolution of the Soul* (Oxford: Clarendon Press, 1986), 11–15.

cognitive, expressibility, and rationality principles. In this section it is the acceptability of the cognitive principle that is under discussion.

### (i) *Swinburne's theory of religious language*

One of the central issues in philosophy of religion has always been how we can speak about God at all. Swinburne's answer is the traditional philosophical answer: literally on most occasions, and analogically on the others. He accepts that we all have an understanding of ordinary language, and argues that the simplest and best way of analysing religious talk is by seeing it as ordinary language applied in a religious sphere. For example, Swinburne asks about believers, 'Why affirm their belief in God as "loving", "creator", "saviour", etc. etc. if these words do not have a similar meaning to their normal meaning?'[4]

The meaning of religious language is different from ordinary language because we cannot always talk of God in exactly the way that we talk of another person. Consequently, we must on occasion use analogy in religious language.[5] We say that God is a Father because he is like human fathers in some, but not all, respects (he cares for his children but he has no sexual partner). None the less, we can use many words of God with the same meaning as in ordinary discourse. To say that God is wise, and that Socrates is wise, applies the same property to God and Socrates; it is simply that God is infinitely wise that provides the difference.

Swinburne refers to the medieval theories of analogy with approval, consciously placing himself in the tradition of Aquinas and Scotus. The doctrine of analogy still holds many adherents in current thinking, particularly the view that believers do use religious language in an analogical manner.[6]

Since it is held that believers do use religious language either literally or analogically, it follows that religious language, like ordinary language, makes assertions about what is and what is not the case. Religious talk about God shows that it is a factual

[4] Richard Swinburne, *The Coherence of Theism* (Oxford: Clarendon Press, 1977), 92–3.                                                                    [5] Ibid. 85.
[6] See e.g. John Hick, *Philosophy of Religion*, 3rd edn. (Englewood Cliffs, NJ: Prentice Hall, 1983), 37–9.

issue, an issue susceptible of truth and falsity, that God exists, that God intervenes in the world, that God created the world, and so on. Swinburne describes this as 'the clear and unambiguous picture of God in the Old and New Testaments, and Jews and Christians have formed their ideas of God by continual study of the Scriptures'.[7]

Behind this account of specifically religious language lies a particular understanding of language and meaning. A statement normally has meaning if it refers, or says something about how things are. Statements cannot have meaning in any other way: performative utterances, for example, do have meaning but they are sentences and not statements, sentences being the general class of which statements are a subset. (In this terminology the mistake of the verificationists was to give meaning only to statements and not to sentences.) For Swinburne, 'A statement, unlike anything else expressed by a sentence, is true or false. Commands, questions, or performative utterances are not true or false.'[8]

This is an understanding of language that has dominated empiricist philosophy. A statement is seen to be true if and only if it corresponds to an actual state of affairs; it is false if it refers to a state of affairs which does not obtain or refers to a true state of affairs in an inaccurate manner. Thus, language about God is assumed to be either true (if it genuinely refers to the way in which God is) or false (if it fails to refer to the way in which God is, or if there is no God to refer to). This is the cognitive principle: that religious statements are true or false, and that truth and falsity apply to statements about God in a similar way to ordinary language.

Swinburne does write that it is 'credal sentences [which] do, as they appear to, make statements',[9] but for him 'God exists' counts as a credal sentence,[10] and therefore the existence of God is susceptible of being true or false. 'God exists' is true if there is an external reality to which the name 'God' corresponds; it is false if there is no such reality. Religious claims are 'claims about a reality beyond the world of sense which accounts for the ordinary things around us'.[11] Either it is true that there is such

[7] Swinburne, *The Coherence of Theism*, 92.    [8] Ibid. 12.
[9] Ibid. 93.    [10] Ibid. 2.    [11] Ibid. 85.

a reality, or it is false. The so-called non-cognitivist theory of religious language (apparently held by thinkers as diverse as Braithwaite, Cupitt, and Phillips), which asserts that the words of religion are merely expressive or exhortative, is universally condemned by traditional philosophy of religion for denying that as a matter of fact either it is true that there is a God or it is false.

The view that language gets its meaning, and statements their truth values, from correspondence to external reality, has a long and respectable historical tradition. It is essentially an empiricist theory of meaning. Hume, for example, held that words have meaning if they relate to a specific idea; and ideas about the world must derive from experience to have any meaning.[12] Wittgenstein, later of course a fervent critic of the correspondence theory of meaning, appears to have provided one of the finest expressions of that very theory in the *Tractatus Logico-Philosophicus*. Richard Rorty, another critic of the theory, writes of the post-Enlightenment obsession with the theory as 'several hundred years of effort [which] have failed to make interesting sense of the notion of "correspondence"'.[13] The vehemence of the attack upon the view that meaning is correspondence to reality in the pragmatist and 'post-Philosophy' movements is an indication of the widespread philosophical acceptance of the theory itself.

For Swinburne, the cognitive nature of religious language is illustrated by an analysis of what believers take their sentences to mean; and what they mean is that God is an external, independent reality to which true religious statements correspond. Obviously not all philosophers accept this, but Swinburne argues that his view would be borne out by 'an extensive sociological and literary survey of what the utterers of theological sentences suppose to be implied by what they say'.[14] Traditional philosophy would concur with Swinburne. John Mackie writes for the tradition with his words, 'the meaning of religious language . . . is very thoroughly and satisfactorily dealt with by Swinburne'.[15]

---

[12] The one exception is abstract ideas of number; see David Hume, *Enquiry Concerning Human Understanding* (1748; Indianapolis: Hackett Publishing Company, 1977).

[13] Richard Rorty, 'Pragmatism and Philosophy', in Kenneth Baynes *et al.* (eds.), *After Philosophy* (1982; London: MIT Press, 1988), 31.

[14] Swinburne, *The Coherence of Theism*, 93.

[15] John Mackie, *The Miracle of Theism* (Oxford: Clarendon Press, 1982), 3.

It is against this whole understanding of language that the Wittgensteinian school has revolted.

Not only does Swinburne have a definite conception of language, he also has a definite conception of religion. It is a conception which espouses the merit of rational support for religious belief and the advantages of reasoning about the existence of God. Wishing to avoid Marxism and Fascism, but to include Buddhism, Swinburne writes that:

I propose to understand by a religion a system which offers what I shall term salvation. . . . I shall understand that a religion offers it if and only if it offers much of the following: a deep understanding of the nature of the world and man's place in it; guidance on the most worthwhile way to live, and an opportunity so to live; forgiveness from God and reconciliation to him for having done what we believed morally wrong; and a continuation and deepening of this well-being in a happy after-life.[16]

Again, this is a conception of religion which fits snugly into traditional philosophy of religion. Most introductions to the subject treat the question of life after death as a factual, verifiable issue, for example, and the optimistic nature of cognitively construed religion is often stressed.[17] The Wittgensteinian school denies not only that life after death means immaterial or physical, verifiable existence after death in this life, and that seeing a cognitively understood salvation is the only ultimately optimistic perspective, but also the whole notion of religion which underlies these types of view. It is to these Wittgensteinian criticisms that I now turn.

### (ii) *Language games and Gallup polls*

It is possible to identify five major criticisms of the traditional account of religious language from within the Wittgensteinian school.

(a) *There is no ordinary language.* The traditional account of religious language argues that we use it because of the similarity

---

[16] Richard Swinburne, *Faith and Reason* (Oxford: Oxford University Press, 1981), 128. I do not feel competent to judge whether or not all forms of Buddhism have actually been included here; but this is not relevant to the present exposition.

[17] See on both points John Hick, *An Interpretation of Religion* (Basingstoke: Macmillan, 1989).

of its words to ordinary language. For Wittgenstein and his followers, however, all language gets its meaning from its own particular context, and thus there is no 'ordinary' language to which other languages must connect. This is brought out in the notion of language games.

For Wittgenstein, language exhibits an ineluctable diversity. Different language games have their own unique grammar and rules for what can and cannot be said, which makes them all distinctive; yet the fact that the same word can be used in different linguistic contexts and yet can often be understood by people involved in a different language game shows that language games are also interconnected.

To understand language, we have to look at it in its own context, and this is what Wittgenstein's notion of language games is trying to emphasize. To assume that a word has an essence (for example, that its essence is to be found in ordinary language) is to impose a single grammar upon a word, which can only lead to misunderstanding of that word's meaning when it is used in other contexts. For example, there is no single meaning of 'rationality' which can be applied to all situations; so to apply the scientific notion of rationality to religion (as traditional philosophy of religion does) is to misunderstand the nature of language.

Wittgenstein is very concerned to deny that language has an essence. For him, words get their meaning as we learn about examples. Thus, in the *Philosophical Investigations*, he writes about the absurdity of an essential meaning of 'green leaf':

If I am shewn various different leaves and told 'This is called a leaf', I get an idea of the shape of a leaf in my mind.—But what does this picture of a leaf look like when it does not shew us any particular shape, but 'What is common to all shapes of leaf'? Which shade is the 'sample in my mind' of the colour green—the sample of what is common to all shades of green?[18]

The same is true of language games. There is no one essence of a game—there is nothing common to ring-a-ring-a-roses and chess—yet the similarities that they share with other examples of what we would call games make us call them games too. There

---

[18] Ludwig Wittgenstein, *Philosophical Investigations*, trans. G. E. M. Anscombe (Oxford: Basil Blackwell, 1953), 34–5.

is no essence of 'language game' because there is no essence of 'language' or 'game'; nevertheless, we can call them all language games because they are linked:

Instead of producing something common to all that we call language, I am saying that these phenomena have no one thing in common which makes us use the same word for all,—but that they are *related* to one another in many different ways. And it is because of this relationship that we call them all 'language'.[19]

The relationships Wittgenstein calls 'family resemblances'. They are what make a word apply in all the contexts in which it does apply, with a different meaning in each context, and yet still be the same word. Thus, language is not arbitrary; our words are closely linked, but not in the way in which traditional philosophy assumes. In other words, in the Wittgensteinian tradition all language gets its meaning from its context, and thus there is no neutral paradigm of language from which religious language might get its meaning.

The consequence of this conception of language is that disputes about a particular sphere should be decided by the internal criteria of that sphere. If two scientists need to decide a scientific issue, then clearly the appropriate language is scientific. If two art critics disagree over the beauty of a painting, the appropriate language is that of aesthetics. Similarly, if two believers disagree over a religious issue, then the appropriate language to use is that of religion.

If, for example, one is faced with two believers and we want to know whether they believe in the same God, we do not need to understand a paradigmatic ordinary language, but specifically religious language in its own context. Rush Rhees[20] makes the point well:

The question whether we mean the same by 'God' may be an important one. It is a question of the role which our statements about God play in

---

[19] Ibid. 31.
[20] Rhees, Norman Malcolm, D. Z. Phillips, and Peter Winch, comprise the group that Alan Keightley calls the 'devout Wittgensteinians', for the reason that 'they either were, like Rhees and Malcolm, Wittgenstein's own students, or because, like Phillips and Winch, they have been closely associated with the independent work of Wittgenstein's pupils'. (Alan Keightley, *Wittgenstein, Grammar and God* (London: Epworth Press, 1976), 12). These are the thinkers whom I have most in mind when I refer to the Wittgensteinians or the Wittgensteinian school.

our worship and in our lives. Or, if we are outside religion and discussing it, the reference is still to the use the language has among those who practise it.[21]

The point that we cannot assess talk about God by any standard external to religious language, such as philosophical reason, has been endorsed by many thinkers outside the Wittgensteinian school as well as inside. D. Z. Phillips writes approvingly of Simone Weil's idea that the only justification of God is his divinity: in other words, that genuine statements about God are genuine by a religious criterion. Barth makes the same point, that what God says is known only in relation to God, not by external means: 'What God utters is never in any way known and true in abstraction from God Himself. It is known and true for no other reason than that He Himself says it, that He in person is in it and accompanies what is said by him.'[22] In short, analysis of religious language shows that its meaning is greatly impoverished and misunderstood if it is subsumed under no more than ordinary, literal statements and analogy.

(b) *Religious language is neither cognitive nor non-cognitive.* Traditional philosophy assumes that language is either cognitive (true or false in the ways in which literal statements are true or false) or non-cognitive (not susceptible of truth or falsity at all). It has ascribed to the Wittgensteinians a non-cognitive theory of religious language since Wittgenstein is clearly opposed to the traditional cognitive theory.

Yet the followers of Wittgenstein want to deny the cognitive or non-cognitive dichotomy. They reject the point that religious language is purely moral exhortation,[23] yet they also want to say that religious language is not true or false in any traditional philosophical sense. Since the idea of language games shows up the diversity of language, it would be absurd to think that the philosophical idea of truth and falsity, which owes much to the kind of truth and falsity concerned with a matter of fact,

---

[21] Rush Rhees, *Without Answers* (London: Routledge and Kegan Paul, 1969), 129–30.

[22] Karl Barth, *Church Dogmatics*, vol. i, pt. 1, trans. G. T. Thomson, 2nd edn. (Edinburgh: T. and T. Clark, 1969), 155.

[23] This distances the Wittgensteinians from the oft-criticized position of R. B. Braithwaite.

is the only kind. Truth and falsity have their home within the religious language game, yet one must understand the form of life of which religion is a part[24] in order to understand the meaning of 'true' and 'false' in language about God.

This can be brought out by considering the difference between the person who denies God and the person who believes in God. For Phillips, the difference between a conceptually unconfused believer and non-believer is not a difference of one finding 'God exists' true and one finding it false because of finding reasons for God's existence convincing or unconvincing. Phillips refers favourably to Wittgenstein's example of someone who believes in the Last Judgement and someone who does not.[25] For Wittgenstein, they are not disagreeing over a matter of fact, a particular issue, one regarding it true and one false; rather, they are expressing different ways of viewing the world. One has room for a picture of the Last Judgement in his life; for the other, the Last Judgement simply has no meaning. Genuine atheism does not find 'God exists' false, as the cognitive principle entails, but meaningless. Genuine agnosticism is not knowing what God means and being unsure whether such a word has an existing referent or not.

The point is made forcefully, for Phillips, in Malcolm's reconstruction of the ontological argument. Malcolm's point is that the argument in *Proslogion III* shows what kind of reality God has, and that for the believer such a God has meaning, while for the atheist such a God has no meaning. Thus Malcolm writes: 'I can imagine an atheist going through the argument, becoming convinced of its validity, actually defending it against objections, yet remaining an atheist.'[26] To think otherwise is to impose the misconceived cognitive principle upon religious language.

*(c) Meaning is use.* The Wittgensteinian school contains a complete repudiation of the traditional philosophical tenet that

---

[24] Religion is often erroneously referred to as a form of life, but in fact, for Wittgenstein, religion could be imagined *in* a form of life.

[25] Ludwig Wittgenstein, *Lectures and Conversations on Aesthetics, Psychology and Religion*, compiled from notes taken by Yorick Smythies *et al.* (Oxford: Basil Blackwell, 1970), 53.

[26] Norman Malcolm, 'Anselm's Ontological Arguments', in D. Z. Phillips (ed.), *Religion and Understanding* (Oxford: Basil Blackwell, 1968), 61.

meaning comes from correspondence to reality. For this school, the meaning of words is the use they are put to in the various contexts in which they find their homes. Language is an activity, and words get their meaning from the practices which give rise to them. For Wittgenstein, it is our ways of life that show what words mean:

> Actually I should like to say that . . . the *words* you utter or what you think as you utter them are not what matters, so much as the difference they make at various points in your life. How do I know that two people mean the same when each says he believes in God? . . . *Practice* gives the words their sense.[27]

In practice, we see that people behave in different ways even in the same context. Therefore, to suppose that the meaning of language could inhere in one property—such as correspondence to reality—is to fail to see the diversity of language games and forms of life.[28] If one looks at such diversity, it is clear for Wittgenstein that many words have so inexact a meaning that they could not correspond to any external reality. He writes of the absurdity of sketching 'a sharply defined picture "corresponding" to a blurred one'.[29] If colours merge into each other without a hint of an outline, no sharp picture can correspond to it. Trying to draw a sharp picture of a blurred one is the same as looking for 'definitions corresponding to our concepts in aesthetics or ethics'[30]—or religion, since ethics and religion share the property of lying at the bounds of language.

The concept of God is such that it is impossible for us to give a clear and distinct description of it. To attempt to do otherwise is to make explicit what should be left vague. To try to give 'God' meaning by equating it with an external reality to which religious language corresponds is to treat God as a scientific, factual entity for which the evidence of philosophical debate can be conclusive.

---

[27] Ludwig Wittgenstein, *Culture and Value*, trans. Peter Winch (Oxford: Basil Blackwell, 1980), 85.

[28] This shadowy expression, which Wittgenstein himself used infrequently, seems to mean something like a context of activity in which language gets its meaning.                      [29] Wittgenstein, *Philosophical Investigations*, 36.

[30] Ludwig Wittgenstein, 'A Lecture on Ethics', MS from notes taken by Friedrich Waismann, in *Philosophical Review*, 74 (1965), 11–12.

For the Wittgensteinians, however, God is part of a world picture, a presupposition and not an inference. The point about world pictures is that it is in them that words get their meaning, and this is true of *all* words. To assume that a world picture could be true or false is to assume that somehow we can get behind presuppositions in order to assess them. As Wittgenstein wrote: 'I have a world picture. Is it true or false? Above all it is the substratum of all my enquiring and asserting.'[31] Since all words get their meaning from our world pictures as they are formed in practical contexts, 'correspondence', 'reality', and so on are no more a test of our language having meaning than any other words or concepts can be. We cannot step outside our language in order to assess it; 'correspondence to reality' is an empty notion in that it implies that we can test the meaning of words by actually checking upon some reality independent of our words. Peter Winch has warned of 'the seductive idea that the grammar of our language is itself the expression of a set of beliefs or theories about how the world is, which might in principle be justified or refuted by an examination of how the world *actually* is'.[32]

This point is not just found in the followers of Wittgenstein we have referred to. Richard Rorty argues that to gloss 'most of the world is as it is whatever we think about it' as 'there is something out there in addition to the world called "the truth about the world"' is to add something that makes no sense. To describe that truth about the world as 'a relation of "correspondence" between certain sentences ... and the world itself' is to say something which no one has ever been able to make sense of.[33]

The Wittgensteinian challenge, then, to traditional philosophy of religion contains the vital point that to see language as gaining meaning by corresponding to external reality misunderstands the entire manner of our coming to use language, and the fact that all our concepts only have their meaning within language.

[31] Ludwig Wittgenstein, *On Certainty*, trans. Dennis Paul and G. E. M. Anscombe (Oxford: Basil Blackwell, 1969), 23.
[32] Peter Winch, 'Language, Belief and Relativism', in H. D. Lewis (ed.), *Contemporary British Philosophy of Religion*, 4th edn. (London: George Allen and Unwin, 1976), 323.                    [33] Rorty, 'Pragmatism and Philosophy', 41.

(*d*) *Meaning is found by grammar, not consensus.* The Wittgen-steinian school emphasizes that philosophers should be concerned with religious and not philosophical language of the wrong sort in order to gain a proper understanding of words about God. The basic idea of the school here is that to find out what 'God' or any other religious word means we must look at the way in which the words are used rather than secondary accounts of their meaning.

We have seen that Swinburne advocates a survey of what believers take themselves to mean by their religious language in order to find out what it does mean. Phillips, however, distin-guishes between a believer's account of prayer, for example, and the prayer itself. We should not expect 'a Gallup poll on people's views about religion', but an exposition of the actual words used in worshipful contexts. A believer might know what he or she is doing when praying, and still be unable to give an account of the prayer. Traditional philosophy of religion has made the mistake of basing its understanding of religious language upon second-ary and largely philosophical accounts rather than the primary language itself. Rush Rhees makes the point thus: 'The question of "what God is" could only be answered through "coming to know God" in worship and in religious life. To know God is to worship him.'[34]

To confuse the apparent similarity of various types of lan-guage with their actual differences is to confuse surface and depth grammar. In Wittgenstein's distinction, surface grammar is how words appear to be on the surface. To say 'There is a table in the room' and 'There is a God in heaven'[35] appear to be very similar; but an analysis of the depth grammar of the words shows them to be very different. Depth grammar is the rules which govern our language in different contexts. It is linked with the practices with which we are involved. Surface grammar is obvious and easy to grasp, but depth grammar requires an understanding of the form of life in which language is used. In Wittgenstein's own words, 'Depth grammar is made explicit by asking what can and what cannot be said of the concept in question. To understand

[34] Rhees, *Without Answers*, 127.
[35] D. Z. Phillips's examples from *Religion and Understanding*, 2.

the limits of what can be said about a concept, one must take account of the context in which the concept is used.'[36]

This Wittgensteinian understanding of how we decide upon the precise meanings of words is in direct opposition to the traditional understanding of looking at believers' accounts of their words instead. This disparity is, I shall argue in Chapter 3, one of fundamental importance in perceiving the limitations of the debate between the Wittgensteinian school and traditional philosophy of religion.

(e) *Religion is a way of life.* Wittgenstein and his followers repudiate the traditional understanding of religion as largely an intellectual assent to a set of propositions held to be true. For Wittgenstein, 'A religious belief could only be something like a passionate commitment to a system of reference. Hence, although it's belief, it's really a way of living, or a way of assessing life. It's passionately seizing hold of this interpretation.'[37] In company with Pascal, Kierkegaard, and much existentialism, Wittgenstein emphasizes the commitment which religion involves. While traditional philosophy concentrates upon the worth of the reasons for belief in God, this alternative school emphasizes that belief in God is not a matter of assessing grounds. Rather, religion is a commitment or entire way of life, a framework *within* which reasons are assessed. Wittgenstein writes that 'Christianity is not a doctrine, not, I mean, a theory about what has happened and will happen to the human soul, but a description of something that actually takes place in human life.'[38] Tolstoy and Dostoevsky, two of Wittgenstein's favourite authors, approved of perceiving religion as a description of a human practice and not as a hypothesis, as did Kierkegaard, some of whose ideas Wittgenstein endorsed, although he claimed not to understand his writings.

The emphasis in all of these writers upon the here-and-now meaning of religion clashes with the traditional philosophical understanding of continued survival in some form of life after death. The same is true of the emphasis upon the practical and presuppositional nature of religion against the traditional

---

[36] Wittgenstein, *Philosophical Investigations*, 168.
[37] Wittgenstein, *Culture and Value*, 64.    [38] Ibid. 30.

philosophical concern with reasons for and against God's existence. Religion is not seen as a system, but as a way of life.
Wittgenstein, echoing Kierkegaard, admits that philosophy of
religion, if it concerns itself with truth and falsity, reasons and
evidence, simply does not fit with Christianity: 'If Christianity
is the truth then all the philosophy that is written about it is
false.'[39]

## 2. THE NATURE OF GOD

### (i) *The traditional philosophical conception of God*

In this section I wish to outline Swinburne's conception of God,
and show how it is the dominant conception of God in traditional
philosophy of religion. The consequence of this conception is that
God is susceptible of justification or falsification; and that therefore the Proofs are appropriate. I shall consider this consequence
in the next chapter.

(a) *God is definable.* Swinburne, in only the second sentence of
his book *The Coherence of Theism*, finds no problem in giving
a definition of the God of theism. '[God is] something like a
"person without a body (i.e. a spirit) who is eternal, free, able to
do anything, knows everything, is perfectly good, is the proper
object of human worship and obedience, the creator and sus-
tainer of the universe."'[40] Much of the rest of his book is spent
rigorously detailing the logical acceptability of this being.

This definition is one which could be found with few vari-
ations in almost any introductory text in the philosophy of religion written in the recent Anglo-American academic environment.
It owes its perhaps most classic formulation to Aquinas,[41] though
God's attributes are well discussed in the generally forgotten
chapters of the *Proslogion* after the ontological argument. It is the
conception which Locke accepts,[42] and which Hume attempts to

---

[39] Ibid. 83.        [40] Swinburne, *The Coherence of Theism*, 1.

[41] Thomas Aquinas, *Summa Theologiae*, trans. Timothy McDermott (Oxford:
Blackfriars, 1963), Ia: 2, 3–11.

[42] John Locke, *An Essay Concerning Human Understanding* (Oxford: Clarendon
Press, 1975), IV. x. 12; p. 625.

refute in *The Dialogues Concerning Natural Religion*. The defender of this traditional conception, Cleanthes, is pilloried by the sceptical Philo, who interestingly concentrates much more of his attack upon Cleanthes than upon Demea, the non-rationalist believer.

This conception of God is usefully referred to as classical theism,[43] thus distinguishing it from and implicitly calling attention to the existence of other types of theism. The variety of theistic beliefs, however, cannot conceal the fact that Western philosophy, at least until the Enlightenment, was largely concerned with classical theism found seminally in Aquinas.

Swinburne accepts that this conception of God found much opposition after the Enlightenment with the sceptical influence of Hume and Kant. Nevertheless, it retains enormous influence over philosophers of religion. Hartshorne and Macquarrie both accept this even though they are concerned to refute the conception. Mackie quotes Swinburne's definition with approval,[44] Hick gives a very similar definition,[45] and it is the conception of God opposed by atheists such as Flew and agnostics such as Kenny. This widespread definition of God depends upon what I call the expressibility principle: that God's attributes are largely expressible and that we can formulate a full enough definition of God to know almost exactly what we believe in or reject.

*(b) God exists or does not exist.* For Swinburne, there is no doubt that either God exists or does not exist, and that human reasoning can decide which. This point has been so uniformly accepted within philosophy of religion that it is hardly stated at all. Hick writes that belief in God logically entails belief that God exists;[46] and Plantinga expresses surprise that anyone could ever doubt this.

*(c) God's existence is a matter of fact.* For Swinburne, and for traditional philosophy of religion as a whole, we can discover whether or not there is a God as we can discover whether or not any particular fact is correct: by weighing and assessing evidence. If one cannot assemble sufficient facts to demonstrate

[43] A term used in e.g. John Macquarrie, *In Search of Deity* (London: SCM Press, 1984). [44] Mackie, *The Miracle of Theism*, 1.
[45] John Hick, *Arguments for the Existence of God* (New York: Herder, 1971), p. vii. [46] Hick, *Philosophy of Religion*, 8.

the probability of God's existence, then there can be no rational belief in him.

Traditional philosophy of religion holds that the primary language of religious belief asserts facts about the world. Hick, for example, writes of 'this deeply ingrained tendency of traditional theism to use the language of fact', and adds that 'traditional Christian and Jewish faith has always presumed the factual character of its basic assertions'.[47]

(d) *God is an explanatory hypothesis.* For Swinburne, we are faced with a variety of competing phenomena—the world itself, contingency, design in nature, the fact of consciousness, morality, miracles, and religious experience—which stand in need of explanation. One of the competing explanations of these phenomena is the existence of God. Belief in God, to be rational, is a hypothesis designed to give the most probable explanation of such phenomena. Swinburne gives the example of God as Creator: 'The vast majority of those who have used religious language have certainly treated the affirmation that God created the world as the confident propounding of a hypothesis explaining its existence.'[48]

This view is widespread in contemporary philosophy of religion. Mackie concurs with Swinburne that the Proofs are rightly interpreted as best explanation arguments;[49] Kenny claims that John of the Cross was misled by his poetic style to underemphasize the role of explanation in theism;[50] Mitchell argues that Christianity 'must be judged by its capacity to make sense of all the available evidence';[51] and Hick asserts that the true task of natural theology is 'to establish both the possibility and the importance (i.e. the *explanatory power*) of the divine existence'.[52]

(e) *God is an inference.* For Swinburne, it is appropriate to conceive of God as a conclusion to an argument or series of

---

[47] Ibid. 94.     [48] Swinburne, *The Coherence of Theism*, 92.

[49] Mackie, *The Miracle of Theism*, 4.

[50] Anthony Kenny, 'Mystical Experience: St. John of the Cross', in Anthony Kenny, *Reason and Religion* (1963; Oxford: Basil Blackwell, 1987), 93.

[51] Basil Mitchell, *The Justification of Religious Belief* (London: Macmillan, 1973), 3.

[52] John Hick, *An Interpretation of Religion* (Basingstoke: Macmillan, 1989), 219.

arguments. Although a common criticism of Aquinas' Five Ways is that the First Cause, Prime Mover, and so on are not equivalent to the God of Christianity, it is generally assumed within traditional philosophy of religion that at least a partial conception of the God of religion can be provided by the Proofs.

(*f*) *God's existence is probable or improbable.* For Swinburne, the Proofs are best construed as attempts to show that it is probable that God exists, while for Mackie they illustrate the improbability of God. Swinburne uses probability calculus, such as Bayes' Theorem, in order to demonstrate his conclusion, while Mackie uses Occam's razor, traditionally conceived,[53] to argue for the improbability of God. The move towards inductive arguments has less of a history than the other points about God's nature, since the Proofs have historically been construed as deductive arguments.

(*g*) *God is an object.* For Swinburne, God is an object, although not in any sense a physical object. Certain implications of the word 'object' cannot be accepted, such as unthinkingness, but

if you mean [by saying of God that he is an object] God is something of which properties are true, which causally interacts with other recognisable observable objects, which can be distinguished from others as the subject of certain predicates which he has and they don't: well, that is the case with God, and therefore on any natural understanding of 'object', God is an object.[54]

Although only implicit in traditional philosophy of religion, it is none the less the case that God is thought of as an object in the above sense. Properties such as omnipotence and immutability are ascribed to God and are uniquely his properties, and God is thought of as making a causal difference to the world (as opposed to deism).

(*h*) *God is comprehensible.* At the root of the traditional conception of God within philosophy of religion, there is the assumption

---

[53] This difference is rarely observed. Swinburne's principle of simplicity looks for the simplest possible final explanation; Mackie's Occam's razor looks for no unwarranted multiplication of entities in an explanation.

[54] Richard Swinburne, in a taped conversation with me at the University of Birmingham, Nov. 1987.

that we can understand God, and that this understanding is through reason. For Swinburne, faith is only relevant when our reason cannot be certain about God, and this happens rarely. We can understand the nature of God by analysing his attributes, and we can understand that he exists by analysing evidence and arguments.

This is the conception of God found generally within Western philosophy, and certainly within such great thinkers as Aquinas, Locke, Descartes, and Kant, and is the object of attack in Hume. For all these thinkers, at least in their more well-known writings, any mysteriousness about God does not interfere with the highly competent ability of the human intellect to understand him.

### (ii) God as mystery

(a) God is inexpressible.    The Wittgensteinian school is wholly opposed not only to the traditional definition of God, but also to the whole idea of any definition of God. Defining God brings him within the boundaries of language rather than allowing him his proper place on the boundaries. To express God is to fail to give due respect to the inexpressible.

As early as the Tractatus, Wittgenstein was aware of the importance of the inexpressible. The book is only a means to see the limits of what can be expressed:

My propositions serve as elucidations in the following way: anyone who understands me eventually recognises them as nonsensical, when he has used them as steps—to climb up beyond them. (He must, so to speak, throw away the ladder after he has climbed up it.) He must surmount these propositions, and then he will see the world aright. What we cannot speak about, we must consign to silence.[55]

The idea that some things can only be shown and not said is central to Wittgenstein. 'What can be shown cannot be said.'[56] The Tractatus is a ladder to be dispensed with once used; it is consideration of the expressible to show how limited the expressible is. Wittgenstein claims that there are two books: the one he could and did write (the Tractatus), and the more important one, the one that he could not write.

[55] Ludwig Wittgenstein, Tractatus Logico-Philosophicus, trans. D. F. Pears and Brian McGuiness (London: Routledge and Kegan Paul, 1961), 6.54–7; p. 151.
[56] Ibid. 4.1212; p. 51.

The inexpressible is revealed in an extra-linguistic way. Wittgenstein describes it as the mystical: 'There are indeed things that cannot be put into words. They make themselves manifest. They are what is mystical.'[57] God is mystical; in other words, we cannot reduce God to words. It is not simply that the traditional philosophical attributes of God have grammatical implications which are incompatible with genuine religious belief (as I shall show in later parts of this section); the point is that any definition of God, any putting of God into words, can only misconceive God, unless the words show up God's inexpressibility.

In order for us to have a conception of the expressible, we must have a conception of the inexpressible also. 'Perhaps what is inexpressible (what I find mysterious and am not able to express) is the background against which what I could express has its meaning.'[58] Since we must have a conception of the inexpressible, it is clear for Wittgenstein that God—who cannot be subsumed under human thought—is a part of the inexpressible. The same is true of ethics and aesthetics: these share with religion the characteristic of showing themselves in the world rather than being fully expressed in language. Religion is not a phenomenon which fits into our usual understanding of what is sensible: rather, it lies beyond the bounds of what we can express in language, and only what we can express in language can be made sense of. To say that religion is nonsense, for Wittgenstein as for Kierkegaard, is not pejorative: rather, it is an emphasis upon the otherness of the God of religion. To define God is to misunderstand this otherness. Thus the Wittgensteinian school opposes the expressibility principle.

(b) *God is not an existent or a being.* The Wittgensteinian school is concerned to show the grammatical inappropriateness of treating God (as traditional philosophy has done) as an existent among existents. Phillips, for example, often quotes Kierkegaard's dictum, 'God does not exist; he is eternal',[59] with approval. The point is that to treat God as an existent is to imply that God might not have existed, and this is clearly not what believers

---

[57] Ibid. 6.522; p. 151.     [58] Wittgenstein, *Culture and Value*, 16.

[59] Søren Kierkegaard, *Concluding Unscientific Postscript*, trans. D. F. Swenson (Princeton, NJ: Princeton University Press, 1941), 296.

have wanted to say at all. For any existing thing, it makes sense to suppose that it might not have existed. All people depend upon their parents having met, and their grandparents, and so on. All living creatures are equally dependent. All man-made objects are dependent for their existence upon a particular person making them in a particular way. A workman made the desk I am working on; it makes perfect sense to suppose that a different desk could have been made. All natural objects depend for their existence upon geographical, geological, and biological factors. The point is that it is to impose an alien grammar upon God to bring him within this realm of discourse. God does not depend for his existence upon anything else; therefore he cannot be described as an existent or being.

This grammatical point is found in all the Wittgensteinians. Rhees explicitly writes that God should not be said to exist, because this implies that God might not have existed;[60] and that if a believer says that God exists, this is not a statement of fact but a confession of faith.[61]

Malcolm is also concerned to deny the relevance of 'existence' to God. He argues that belief that God exists is *not* a religious belief; because the existence of $x$ can be determined in principle by reference to facts and evidence; whereas the appropriate response to God is an affective one. To say that God exists distorts the impossibility of believing in God and yet being indifferent to God. Thus the grammar of existence is seriously misleading when applied to God.

Phillips makes much use of Malcolm's paper on the ontological argument. He agrees with Malcolm's central insight that Anselm has revealed that it is grammatically mistaken to speak of God as an existent, because of the implication of contingency entailed by our usual notion of existence. Necessary 'existence' is grammatically apposite, because it allows for God's eternity. God is unlimited, not a being. 'Malcolm . . . succeeds in showing that the most important idea of God in Hebrew and Christian traditions is an idea of unlimited being, necessary existence, and so on.'[62] Despite protestations by Swinburne,[63] Hick,[64] and others that they

[60] Rhees, *Without Answers*, 116.     [61] Ibid. 132.

[62] D. Z. Phillips, *The Concept of Prayer* (New York: Schocken Books, 1966), 82.

[63] See Swinburne, *The Coherence of Theism*, 254–80.

[64] See Hick, *Philosophy of Religion*, 7–9.

do discuss a necessarily existent God, the Wittgensteinian school holds that to treat God as susceptible of evidence and reasoning, as expressible and factual, is to treat God in practice as existing contingently.

In this century in particular there has been much thought about Being, or Being-itself. Heidegger writes much about Being, and Tillich equates God with Being, or the ground of Being, not as a being. The intention behind this is to remove God from the order of beings, of which God is not seen as a part. God is of a different logical order from existents.

Finally, there is a moral objection to seeing God as an existent. Phillips, following Wittgenstein, sees theodicies as morally and grammatically misconceived projects to justify God in the face of evil. If God is of the order of beings, then evil is an overwhelming moral objection to God. God cannot be an existent, because, if he were, he would be morally culpable for evil. Wittgenstein, in the vein of Ivan Karamazov, refuses to worship such a God.[65]

(c) *God is not a matter of fact.* It is just as grammatically confused to treat God as a fact as to treat God as an existent, and for the same reason. Facts are contingent: they are true, but they might not have been. God, however, cannot be spoken of as existing contingently, and this means that we cannot speak of God's reality as factual. Facts can change: we can come to find that, because of new evidence, what we thought of as a fact was mistaken. Yet it makes no sense to say that belief in God was mistaken because new facts have been discovered to show this. To come to believe in God, for Phillips, is not to discover a new fact—that there is a God—but to change one's life in a fundamental and practical manner. A God who is factual, 'a God who is an existent among existents is not the God of religious belief'.[66]

(d) *God is practical, not hypothetical.* The Wittgensteinian school rejects the notion that God is an explanation of life in the way that a hypothesis is. If new evidence comes to light to show that the Big Bang theory, or neo-Darwinian evolution, is true, this

---

[65] M. C. O'Drury, 'Conversations with Wittgenstein', in Rush Rhees (ed.), *Recollections of Wittgenstein* (Oxford: Oxford University Press, 1984), 107–8.

[66] Phillips, *The Concept of Prayer*, 81.

does not alter the genuine religious belief in God. God is not an explanation, because God is not in competition with any explanatory theory. Losing belief in God because of scientific advance reveals an inadequate conception of God.

Similarly, genuine belief in God is not hypothetical or theoretical. To treat God as a hypothesis is to believe in God tentatively; new evidence could at any time arise to show that our hypothesis was mistaken. We would have to check scientific and philosophical journals regularly to ensure that our belief in God was still rational.

In the Wittgensteinian school, God is a practical, not theoretical, entity. Peter Winch writes that what God's reality 'amounts to can only be seen from the religious tradition in which the concept of God is used, and this is unlike the use of scientific concepts, say of theoretical entities'.[67] Genuine believers do not give up their beliefs in the way in which beliefs in hypotheses are given up.

Construing God as an explanatory hypothesis leaves out the essential element of belief in God, namely commitment. Kierkegaard, for example, writes of having an infinite passion, a full commitment to God. This commitment is an utterly consuming and life-transforming affair, unlike any belief in an explanatory hypothesis.

(e) *God is not an inference, but a presupposition.*   For a Proof of God to be an appropriate task, it must be grammatically and religiously acceptable to be able to treat God, at least in part, as an inference from an idea of unsurpassable perfection, facts about the world, or the existence of the world itself. Phillips opposes such a view by arguing that God is an ungrounded presupposition in the believer's world-view. God is not to be inferred, but things are to be inferred from God.

God, for Wittgenstein, is a measure or yardstick, not something to be inferred from some other measure such as philosophical reasoning. Belief in God is the undergirding of a way of looking at the world, not the result of simply looking at the world and then trying to explain it. Religious belief is too fundamental and all-encompassing to be able to base it upon external factors.

[67] Peter Winch, 'Understanding a Primitive Society', *American Philosophical Quarterly*, i (1964), 309.

Kierkegaard makes the point that faith is a leap which begins precisely at the moment at which reason, thought, and inference cease to be appropriate. Wittgenstein makes the similar point that God lies at the limits of language; it is therefore absurd to suppose that we could infer God from anything expressible in language. For both thinkers, belief in God is a presupposition of a way of life only possible if one is aware of the limits of inference. Karl Barth concurs, arguing that genuine faith (for him, evangelical faith) must presuppose and not infer God's reality: 'The faith which is engaged with struggling with doubt about the truth, struggling with the question, Is there a God? is a different one from the faith in which man asks whether God, whose existence is not a problem, is gracious to him, or whether man must despair of himself.'[68]

(*f*) *God is neither probable nor improbable.* Phillips ridicules the traditional philosophy of religion for supposing that believers hold God's reality to be probable and that unbelievers hold God's reality to be improbable. In his article 'The Friends of Cleanthes', Phillips accuses Swinburne of being a believer, and Mackie an unbeliever, in the style of Hume's traditional theist, Cleanthes. Phillips writes scathingly, 'If religious beliefs are matters of probability, should we not reformulate religious beliefs so that the natural expression of them becomes less misleading? Should we not say from now on, "I believe it is highly probable that there is an almighty God, maker of heaven and earth."?'[69] In this he is following Wittgenstein, who scornfully suggested that Augustine might not have accepted that the existence of God was highly probable. The point is that belief in God is a fundamental attitude to life, not a juggling of probabilities: this is why Pascal's Wager has seemed to many to be an impossible way to come to God.[70]

Kierkegaard even stresses that, by purely human reason, the existence of God, and particularly the incarnation, which he calls

[68] Barth, *Church Dogmatics*, vol. i, pt. 1, p. 38.

[69] D. Z. Phillips, 'The Friends of Cleanthes', *Modern Theology*, i/2 (Jan. 1985), 91–2.

[70] This misunderstands Pascal somewhat: the Wager is deliberately aimed at a pragmatic group who have certain already established presuppositions which Pascal is playing upon.

the 'paradox', are simply absurd. They are opposed to the exercise of reason in the pursuit of probable conclusions. Probability is linked to reason, which is simply a lower attitude to life than faith, which eschews matters of probability. The point was well made before Kierkegaard by Pascal: 'Who then will condemn Christians for being unable to give rational grounds for their belief, professing as they do a religion for which they cannot give rational grounds? They declare that it is a folly, *stultitiam*, in expounding it to the world.'[71]

(g) *God is not an object.*  The Wittgensteinian school finds another grammatical mistake in traditional philosophy of religion here. For this tradition there is a grammatical difference between talking about objects and talking about God. To ask if two people mean the same thing when they speak of God can only be discovered by examining their religious life. On the other hand, to find out if two people mean the same when they are referring to what is apparently the same object, we would investigate the object itself and try to discover things about it. Rhees makes the point forcefully by arguing that empirical type criteria are appropriate to a difference of opinion about an object, and adds:

But the question whether we mean the same by God . . . is not a question whether we are referring to the same object. The question whether we are still talking about God now, or whether we are really worshipping God now, cannot be settled by referring to any object. And I do not think it would mean anything to ask 'whether any such object exists'.[72]

A disagreement about an object is a difference of opinion, and can be resolved empirically; but a disagreement about the nature or reality of God is a fundamental divergence in ways of life, and thus is very different from opposing opinions. Talk of God is grammatically disparate from talk of objects; hence to talk of God as an object is misconceived.

(h) *God is supernatural, not natural.*  The Wittgensteinian school is concerned to place mystery and incomprehensibility in its appropriate place in religion. For Phillips, expounding Kierkegaard,

---

[71] Pascal, *Pensées*, trans. A. Krailsheimer (Harmondsworth: Penguin, 1985), 150.
[72] Rhees, *Without Answers*, 131.

God is not mysterious because we do not yet know enough about him, but will (perhaps in some 'eschatological verification', to use Hick's phrase); rather, understanding God is to understand that we cannot ever understand him. This is the genuinely religious understanding of God's mystery.

The Wittgensteinian school stresses the incomprehensibility of God in the face of the comprehensibility of the God of the traditional philosophy of religion. The former Phillips describes as the supernatural God, the latter as the natural God. In this he follows Simone Weil, who is concerned to safeguard what she sees as the proper Christian understanding of God:

Like a gas, the soul tends to fill the entire space which is given it. A gas which contracted leading to a vacuum—this would be contrary to the law of entropy. It is not so with the God of the Christians. He is a *supernatural* God, whereas Jehovah is a *natural* God.[73]

For Weil, Jehovah is a partial, parochial God; the God of Christianity transcends partiality and is therefore supernatural. Human beings reflect this distinction in their motives for actions. In the giving of alms, for example, if we give to make ourselves feel better, or to demonstrate our goodness, then we are performing a natural act; whereas if we act out of genuine compassion for the poor, we have performed a supernatural act.

The God of traditional philosophy of religion is a natural God, because it depends upon human reasoning and human justification for its reality. All the grammatical objections against this God brought by the Wittgensteinian school are designed to show that this natural God is not the God of religious belief. It neither conforms to what believers mean when they talk to and of God in prayer and worship, nor are its grammatical implications those of the God of religion. In short, the Wittgensteinian school accuses traditional philosophy of religion of discussing a natural and not a supernatural God.

[73] Simone Weil, *Gravity and Grace*, trans. Emma Craufurd (London: Routledge and Kegan Paul, 1958), 43.

# 2

# The Proper Role of Philosophy

In this chapter I will deal with the traditional philosophical acceptance of, and rejection of, what I will call the principle of rationality. This states that the issue of the existence of God is susceptible of philosophical justification or refutation (or simply agnosticism if the arguments and evidence examined are inconclusive). The principle assumes that reason can be usefully applied to discussion of God's existence, and that it is an appropriate philosophical task to attempt to justify or refute objects the existence of which is contentious.

I will show in Section 1 that Swinburne stands in a long tradition, still dominant today, of holding to the rationality principle. In Section 2 I shall contrast his position with that of Phillips in particular, showing how the Wittgensteinians also stand in a long tradition of rejecting the rationality principle. Finally, in Section 3, I shall apply my discussion to the appropriateness of the Proofs themselves.

## 1. THE POWER OF REASON

### (i) *Swinburne's project*

The second volume of Swinburne's trilogy, entitled *The Existence of God*, is an attempt to show that it is probable that God exists, and that therefore we are rationally compelled to believe in God. Swinburne argues that a cumulative case can be made for God's existence using the evidence available from all the classical *a posteriori* Proofs. The versions of the ontological argument are rejected as being 'mere philosophers' arguments' which do not reflect the reasons of ordinary men for believing in God: moreover, 'the greatest theistic philosophers of religion have on the whole rejected ontological arguments and have relied instead on *a posteriori* ones'.[1]

Swinburne's originality lies in rejecting deductive arguments for God's existence (because naturalism is not incoherent and because no deductively valid argument in this sphere begins with generally accepted premisses) and replacing them with inductive arguments. A good C-inductive argument is one which makes the conclusion more probable than it would otherwise be, while a good P-inductive argument makes the conclusion more probable than not.

The traditional *a posteriori* arguments for God's existence, the cosmological, teleological, and moral, and the less traditional arguments from consciousness, providence, history, and miracles, only provide a weak C-inductive conclusion that God exists. The only proper way to assess religion and science, as competing hypotheses to explain these phenomena, is by using some version of Occam's razor, or what Swinburne calls the principle of simplicity: 'In a given field, we take as most likely to be true the simplest theory which fits best with other theories of neighbouring fields to produce the simplest set of theories of the world.'[2] The prior probability of any hypothesis explaining the phenomena which we do encounter, which otherwise would be highly unlikely, is the simplicity of that hypothesis.

For Swinburne, religion is inherently simple, for God is the most simple being that there could possibly be. There is no complexity in his nature: all the attributes which he possesses are total in their capacity. Whereas human beings are sometimes good and sometimes bad, God is always completely good; whereas human beings know some things and not others, God knows everything that can be known; and so on. Furthermore, whereas naturalism must posit both scientific explanation (explanation by natural laws or objects) and personal explanation (explanation by beliefs, intentions, and capacities of the agent), theism need only posit personal explanation as ultimate: all is owing to God's agency. Having one irreducible type of explanation is simpler than having two, and God is the most simple being possible; therefore, although theism, like naturalism, does

---

[1] Richard Swinburne, *The Existence of God* (Oxford: Oxford University Press, 1979), 10.      [2] Swinburne, *The Evolution of the Soul*, 13.

not make the existence of the phenomena of the world, phenomena which 'cry out for explanation',[3] very likely, it makes them
more likely than any other hypothesis does.

The crucial phenomenon is that of religious experience. Given
that theism and naturalism explain other phenomena equally
well, what is required is the simplest possible explanation of
religious experience, and this is provided by the existence of
God. The argument from religious experience, in Swinburne,
depends upon two principles: those of credulity and testimony.
The principle of credulity states 'that (in the absence of special
considerations) things are (probably) as others are inclined to
believe that they have perceived them',[4] while the principle of
testimony states 'that (in the absence of special considerations)
the experiences of others are (probably) as they report them'.[5]

Special considerations do apply in some cases: for example,
if the witness had been drinking heavily, or is known to be a
habitual liar. However, when these considerations do not apply,
application of the principles of credulity, testimony, and simplicity show that God is the best explanation of religious experience, and that therefore we are rationally compelled to believe in
him. All other evidence for and against God's existence is
inconclusive (the argument of the rest of *The Existence of God*), and
the concept of God is coherent (the argument of *The Coherence
of Theism*); therefore, the argument from religious experience is
decisive.

Thus we can see philosophical reasoning at work in reaching
a conclusion about the existence of God. In his introductory remarks in *The Existence of God*, Swinburne suggests that such a
project has an overwhelming historical precedent:

[I hold a] deep conviction of the possibility of reaching fairly well
justified conclusions by argument on this issue.... It is a conviction
which was explicitly acknowledged by the vast majority of Christian (and
non-Christian) philosophers from the thirteenth to the eighteenth
centuries; and, I believe, shared, although less explicitly, by many
Christian (and non-Christian) philosophers from the first to the twelfth
centuries.[6]

---

[3] Swinburne, *The Existence of God*, 290.     [4] Ibid. 272.
[5] Ibid.     [6] Ibid. 1–2.

It is not hard to find thinkers who support Swinburne's contention. Aquinas is an example of the typical medieval trust in philosophical reasoning concerning the existence of God. He refers favourably to Romans 1: 20 ('the hidden things of God can be clearly understood from the things that he has made'), and concludes from a discussion of different types of demonstration that 'from effects evident to us, therefore, we can demonstrate what in itself is not evident to us, namely, that God exists'.[7] This principle underlies Aquinas' arguments for God's existence, contained in the Five Ways. Indeed, it is still standard Catholic teaching that, in the words of Pius XII, 'human reason can, without the help of divine revelation and grace, prove the existence of a personal God by arguments drawn from created things'.[8] Anselm too seemed to place a great trust in reasoning about God's existence in his ontological argument,[9] and Locke, although holding some beliefs to be above the power of reason (such as belief in the resurrection of the dead), firmly places belief in God under the grouping of beliefs according to reason.[10]

As we have seen already, Swinburne accepts that the sceptical attitude of Hume and Kant has caused post-Enlightenment doubts about the efficacy of philosophical reasoning about God. Descartes certainly is a paradigm example of a thinker committed to the susceptibility of God's existence to reason; and it is against thinkers like him that Hume launches his attack in the *Dialogues*. The non-rationalist believer, Demea, is given cursory treatment, and Philo speaks for Cleanthes as well as himself with the dictum, 'if we distrust human Reason, we have no other principles to lead us into Religion'.[11]

Nevertheless, Swinburne sees Hume and Kant as having bequeathed the kind of distrust of reasoning about religion which Kierkegaard and Wittgenstein (at least on Swinburne's reading of them) endorse. His response to this is to argue that the discoveries of modern science cast considerable doubt upon the

[7] Thomas Aquinas, *Summa Theologiae*, I: 2, 2, p. 11.
[8] Papal Encyclical 'Humani Generis' (1940), esp. paragraphs 2, 3, 25, 29. Quoted in John Hick (ed.), *The Existence of God*, p. 20.
[9] Although we must be careful in interpreting Anselm: see my Ch. 6, Sect. 3.
[10] Locke, *An Essay Concerning Human Understanding*, IV.vii.23; p. 687.
[11] David Hume, *Dialogues Concerning Natural Religion* (Oxford: Clarendon Press, 1935), 172.

assumption common to Hume and Kant that we can know little beyond immediate experience. For example, in response to Hume and Kant's principle that the cause of one observable phenomenon must be another observable phenomenon, Swinburne points to the 'evident success of chemistry and physics in providing good grounds to believe in the existence of atoms, electrons, photons etc.'.[12] Rational justification applies far more widely than those who seminally opposed it thought; thus, there is no ground from Hume or Kant's reasoning to suppose that rational justification cannot apply to the existence of God.

There are five points made explicitly in Swinburne's writings, and three points made more generally in traditional philosophy of religion, which are designed to show why the Proofs are an appropriate and also commendable approach to God's existence, and it is to these that I now turn.

### (ii) *Cognitive assumptions*

(*a*) It is important, according to Swinburne, for a believer to know whether God really exists or is simply a figment of the imagination. He writes that 'you can only have a personal relationship to God in Christ, if it is true that God exists'.[13] One of the ways of determining whether or not God exists is by philosophical reasoning. This point is made in opposition to the strain in Protestant thinking which emphasizes a personal relationship to God above rational justification of God, as in Barth and early Bultmann.

(*b*) It is a duty for Christians to convert others, and, for Swinburne, one means of conversion would be by rational argument, just as rational argument can be seen to play a significant role in altering someone's mind on most issues of importance.

(*c*) One can be confused or mistaken about beliefs which one holds very closely; therefore, in the face of criticisms from non-believers, Swinburne writes that 'it is no bad thing to check your claim by considering whether their objections provide you with grounds for sharing their scepticism'.[14]

---

[12] Swinburne, *The Existence of God*, 54 n. 2.
[13] Swinburne, *The Coherence of Theism*, 6.    [14] Ibid.

(*d*) For Swinburne, true belief is inherently important, and one gains true belief by having rationally justified belief. It is only by holding true beliefs that man can reach his ends and purposes; and, furthermore, true belief is a constituent of knowledge and knowledge itself is valuable.

(*e*) The issue of God's existence is so important that it is unusually vital to hold a true belief about it; and one way of coming to hold true beliefs is by checking that rational justification is necessary for true belief in God. In Aquinas, for example, it is clear that philosophical reasoning is not required for a genuine belief in God: 'There is nothing to stop a man accepting on faith some truth which he personally cannot demonstrate, even if that truth in itself is such that demonstration could make it evident.'[15] However, modern thinkers such as Kenny and Mackie find it impossible that belief not susceptible of proof or disproof could be acceptable. For them—and this is not the case for many cognitivists, including Hick, Mitchell, and Plantinga—rational justification is not only appropriate but also necessary if religious belief is to have any genuine worth.

(*f*) For Kenny in particular, faith is a whimsical vice unless supported by the virtue of reason. A rational belief is virtuous because it is well grounded; a non-rational belief is vicious because it has no good grounding and is therefore arbitrary. Kenny concludes that 'if the validity or invalidity of arguments for and against the existence of God is wholly irrelevant to faith, then faith seems a vicious habit of mind, a turning of one's back on the possibility of discovering truth'.[16]

This point is at least implicitly endorsed by most Enlightenment and post-Enlightenment philosophers of religion who would fit under the term cognitive, such as Descartes, Hume, and, most eloquently, Locke:

He that believes, without having any Reason for believing, may be in love with his own fancies; but neither seeks Truth as he ought, nor pays

[15] Thomas Aquinas, *Summa Theologiae*, I: 2, 2, p. 11.
[16] Anthony Kenny, *The God of the Philosophers* (Oxford: Clarendon Press, 1979), 128.

the Obedience due his Maker. . . . For he governs his Assent right, and places it as he should, who in any Case or Matter whatsoever, believes or disbelieves according as Reason directs him.[17]

The Proofs are important and appropriate to belief in God because they are the classical means of trying to make belief in God more than a whim by giving it a solid rational foundation.

(*g*) The major alternative for grounding belief in God other than reason is revelation; and for traditional philosophy of religion, revelation itself should be subject to rational justification. Again, this is a point which is echoed by Locke, and is made forcefully in modern times, in the face of Barth and similar thinkers who place revelation prior to reason, by Flew, Mackie, and Kenny, for example. Kenny writes that 'Faith is believing something on the word of God; and one cannot take God's word for it that He exists. Belief in God's existence must be logically prior to belief in revelation.'[18]

We cannot accept a revelation as coming from God without further grounds, because the guarantee that we have of the revelation being from God is God himself, and this is clearly circular. Therefore, man must exercise his reason in deciding whether a revelation is really from God or not. Philosophical reasoning about God's existence is important because it, and not revelation, is prior.

(*h*) One role of philosophy, for traditional philosophers of religion, is to justify or refute objects the existence of which is contentious. There is seen to be a need to justify the existence of God because there is so much disagreement about whether or not God exists. Philosophy may not be able to determine whether or not tables exist—indeed, it is a notorious point in philosophy that we cannot justify the existence of the external world—yet in cases such as these there is no need to. No sane person doubts the existence of tables, but plenty of sane people doubt that there is a God; hence the need for a philosophical justification of God's existence.

---

[17] Locke, *An Essay Concerning Human Understanding*, iv.vii; p. 687.
[18] Anthony Kenny, *A Path from Rome* (London: Sidgwick and Jackson, 1985), 147.

This conception of philosophy is a highly positive one. Kenny urges philosophers of religion to 'go on the offensive' and prove or disprove the existence of God;[19] Hick writes that 'philosophical considerations are relevant to a decision as to whether or not it is reasonable to believe that God exists';[20] and for Plantinga 'the main function of apologetics is to show that from a philosophical point of view, Christians and other theists have nothing whatever for which to apologise'.[21] The idea of philosophy being able to prove or disprove the existence of God underpins Swinburne's whole project, Mackie's response, and large parts of most introductions to philosophy of religion. It is against such a picture of the proper role of philosophy, and the principle of rationality in general, that the Wittgensteinian school rebels.

## 2. THE LIMITS OF REASON

### (i) *Religious issues*

One of the central themes of Wittgensteinian thinking is that a religious issue such as the reality of God cannot be determined by criteria external to religion. Philosophical justification of God's reality is a stringent example of a kind of discourse illicitly impinging upon a quite different kind of discourse. Swinburne, in his second and third points, writes as if attempting to convince someone of the truth of Christianity, or attempting to rebut charges against Christianity, is something a philosopher *qua* philosopher can properly do.

Now, Phillips does not want to say that a philosopher can say nothing about religion. We shall see later that philosophy's role, for Phillips, is one of describing religious language and clearing up any grammatical confusions in *philosophical* accounts of religion.

Religious language has its own particular grammar, as any kind of discourse has, and it is only by using that grammar that

---

[19] Anthony Kenny, 'In Defence of God', *TLS* (7 Feb. 1975), 145.
[20] John Hick, *God and the Universe of Faiths* (London: Macmillan Press, 1973), 29.
[21] Alvin Plantinga, 'Self-Profile', in James Tomberlin and Peter van Inwagen (eds.), *Alvin Plantinga* (Dordrecht: Boston Publishing Co., 1985), 93.

one can solve (or see the impossibility of solving) religious issues. We have seen earlier how, for writers such as Rhees and
Phillips, coming to see that God is real, or not real, is a matter of
purely religious language. The attempt by philosophy to justify
the reality of God is much the same as a philosophical justification of a scientific hypothesis or the beauty of a painting: clearly
these are issues which depend upon the criteria of science and
aesthetics respectively. To see God as needing rational justification,
and failing to believe in him if it cannot be found, is the same
kind of category mistake as scorning a scientist for not painting
enough pictures.

The mistake of traditional philosophy of religion is to assume
that we can talk about the rationality of belief in God as if rationality means the same in all contexts. It was exactly this sort of
mistake which the later Wittgenstein attempted to bring to light;
and both Barth and Kierkegaard argue against religion submit-
ting to the external conception of rationality imposed by philosophy. Barth, for example, writes that 'The criterion of Christian
language, in past and future, as well as at the present time, is thus
the essence of the Church, which is Jesus Christ'.[22] It is remark-
able how many attempts are made to justify the existence of the
God of Christianity by rational means in a manner completely
divorced from consideration of the role of Christ in Christian
belief.

### (ii) *God and justification*

Swinburne's other three points all require that it is important,
and appropriate, to be able to justify God's existence. If God
cannot be justified, he must be a figment of the imagination;
if belief in general is to be true, it must be rationally justified;
and if belief in God in particular is to be true, it too must be
rationally justified. The Wittgensteinian school finds an over-
emphasis upon the power of philosophical reasoning in all three
assumptions.

First, writers such as Phillips reject the dichotomy of God
either being rationally justifiable or a mental figment. This point
will be examined in more detail in the next chapter, but it is

---

[22] Barth, *Church Dogmatics*, vol. i, pt. 1, p. 3.

important to notice here that philosophy is in error if it imposes an alien set of options upon a particular discourse. To say that numbers have justifiable existence, or that they have only mental existence, is to impose an alien dichotomy upon the mathematical reality of numbers. It is to fail to take into account that reality does not mean the same in each context. Thus to assume that God is either a product of the imagination or a rationally justifiable being is to impose a mistaken and pre-decided philosophical dichotomy upon the reality of God.

Secondly, to see true belief as that which is rationally justified is to impose a unitary grammar upon the notion of truth. To hold that it is true that I am called Richard Messer is not to hold this on the basis of evidence. My name being what it is, is so fundamental for me that rational justification could not make it more certain. The beliefs that there is an external world and that there are other minds are equally fundamental. Thus not all true beliefs can be rationally justified.

This also applies, thirdly, to belief in the reality of God. Belief in God is what Malcolm, following Wittgenstein, calls a 'groundless belief'. This means that it is a fundamental presupposition for the believer, a yardstick by which other beliefs can be measured. It is not itself measured by reference to evidence or reasons behind it; it lies at a level below evidential and rational support.

Kierkegaard, Wittgenstein, and Barth were appalled by the idea that man could justify God, and this opposition to overconfidence in human reasoning is evident in the Wittgensteinians. Thus Malcolm relates how Wittgenstein applauded Kierkegaard:

He [Wittgenstein] was impatient with 'proofs' of the existence of God, and with attempts to give religion a *rational* foundation. When I once quoted to him Kierkegaard to this effect: 'How can it be that Christ does not exist, since I know that He has saved me?', Wittgenstein exclaimed: 'You see! It isn't a matter of *proving* anything!'[23]

Malcolm has expanded at some length upon the idea that belief in God does not stand in need of justification in his paper 'The Groundlessness of Belief', in which he argues that belief in God underpins the religious language game, and that justification only

[23] Norman Malcolm, *Ludwig Wittgenstein: A Memoir* (London: Oxford Unversity Press, 1958), 71.

makes sense *within* a language game. It is impossible to justify
the language game and its fundamental beliefs (such as belief in
the reality of God), whether by philosophy or by any other means.
Phillips is not alone in quoting Malcolm's remarks on this area
with approval.[24]

We can see how these comments also react against the position
of philosophers like Kenny for whom faith without reason is
a vicious whim. Faith in God simply comes before the level at
which (philosophical) justification becomes relevant; and if this
makes faith vicious, then so are beliefs in the external world. To
assume that every belief needs justifying shows a misunderstanding of when justification comes to an end; and to assume
that belief in God needs justifying is to misunderstand the level
at which belief in God lies.

The Bible is certainly unconcerned with any request to provide
a rational justification of God, prompting Malcolm's remark:
'Someone whose religious concepts were formed exclusively from
the Bible might regard this question of evidence as an alien in-
trusion. It would have no contact with the religion that he had
learned.'[25]

### (iii) *God and reason*

For the Wittgensteinian school, the claim that revelation stands
in need of rational justification demonstrates an arrogant confidence in the powers of philosophical reason. To argue that reason is capable of judging conclusively whether or not a revelation
is from God is to see reasoning about God as having limitations
rather than limits. Phillips, in his paper 'On Not Understanding
God', argues that we do not have limitations, meaning constraints
that could theoretically be overcome, in our understanding of
and reasoning about God, but limits, meaning constraints that it
makes no sense to suppose that we could overcome. The mystery of God is not that we know certain things about him and his
revelation, and could come to full understanding, but that we
know God when we realize that we cannot know him.

To assume that such mystery should be subject to reason is to

[24] D. Z. Phillips, *Faith after Foundationalism* (London: Routledge, 1988), 126.
[25] Norman Malcolm, 'Is it a Religious Belief that God Exists?', in John Hick
(ed.), *Faith and the Philosophers* (London: Macmillan, 1964), 108.

elevate reason above faith, something which Kierkegaard accused Hegel of. Phillips quotes Kierkegaard with approval: 'Suppose Christianity never intended to be understood. . . . Suppose it refuses to be understood and that the maximum of understanding which could come into question is to understand that it cannot be understood.'[26] Philosophical reasoning simply cannot take the God of Christianity within its aegis. The incarnation, for example, is for Kierkegaard an offence against human reasoning. For reason, God and man being combined is a paradox which cannot be resolved. Accepting the paradox for what it is involves seeing the limits of philosophical reasoning. Therefore, to attempt to use reason to determine whether or not God exists is both misconceived and ridiculous. 'For the fool says in his heart that there is no God, but he who says in his heart or to others: Just wait a little and I shall demonstrate it—oh, what a rare wise man he is! What a superb theme for crazy comedy.'[27]

Kierkegaard is not opposed to reason *per se*—he does, after all, use reason to support his own position—merely reason when it goes beyond its own limits. To use reason on issues susceptible of reason is a good thing: but to use reason on issues such as the existence of God is to go beyond reason's limits. The illicit use of reason is one of the major targets of the first existentialists like Pascal and Kierkegaard, influential Protestant thinkers like Barth and Bultmann, and the whole Wittgensteinian school. Pascal, for example, wrote: 'Reason's last step is the recognition that there are an infinite number of things which are beyond it. It is merely feeble if it does not go as far as to realize that.'[28]

### (iv) *Philosophy as description*

The final point made in the list of the assumptions of cognitive philosophy of religion is that philosophy's role is justifying or refuting objects the existence of which is contentious. Having seen how the school in which Phillips stands rejects the principle of rationality because of the limits of reason and the consequent

---

[26] Kierkegaard, *Concluding Unscientific Postscript*, 191.

[27] Søren Kierkegaard, *Philosophical Fragments*, trans. D. F. Swenson (Princeton, NJ: Princeton University Press, 1985), 43.

[28] Blaise Pascal, *Pensées* (1659), trans. A Krailsheimer (Harmondsworth: Penguin, 1985), 85.

limited role of philosophical justification, we must now see what
Phillips would put in its place.

Wittgenstein's conception of philosophy, faithfully endorsed
by his followers, is that philosophy's role is description rather
than justification. The grammatical difference between philosophy and religion, and the groundless nature of belief in God,
means that philosophy can only describe the way in which religious language is used in its context, and point out the grammatical errors in confused philosophical descriptions of religion.

Phillips quotes with approval Wittgenstein's image of traditional philosophy being the fly in the fly-bottle. All that can be
done to escape is to go back the way that one has come; in other
words, to turn one's back on the traditional philosophical enterprise of justification. Winch emphasizes that philosophy 'is a
matter of tracing the implications of the concepts we use',[29] while
Rhees notes approvingly that 'Wittgenstein would have demol-
ished, if he could, the idea of philosophical discussion as a contest to settle who's right and who's wrong'.[30] Finally, Malcolm
uses Wittgenstein's own metaphor to show how philosophy only
removes confusions and does not provide anything new:
'Philosophical work of the right sort merely unties knots in
our understanding. The result is not a theory but simply—
no knots!'[31] Thus, the Wittgensteinians concur in construing
philosophy as conceptual elucidation and grammatical clarification, not as justification and proof.

By misconstruing the nature of philosophy, traditional philosophers have created sham problems, such as the logical validity
of the Proofs. Purely philosophical problems cannot be allowed
to masquerade as religious ones. The traditional philosophical
temptation to make religion into a rationally grounded system is
one to be resisted, because it misconceives both religion and
philosophy.

Swinburne and cognitive philosophers in general seem to want
to construe philosophy as a neutral activity which is, at least
largely, independent of the philosopher. For the Wittgensteinians,

[29] Peter Winch, *The Idea of a Social Science* (London: Routledge and Kegan Paul,
1958), 18.

[30] Rush Rhees, 'The Philosophy of Wittgenstein', in *Discussions of Wittgenstein*
(London: Routledge and Kegan Paul, 1970), 42.

[31] Norman Malcolm, *Problems of Mind* (London: Allen and Unwin, 1976), p. xi.

however, the religious insights which a philosopher possesses
(or lacks) are bound to affect his or her description of religious
language. For Wittgenstein himself, philosophy is a battle for
change within oneself. 'Working in philosophy—like working
in architecture in many respects—is really more a working on
oneself. On one's own interpretation. On one's way of seeing
things. (And what one expects of them.)'[32]

Simone Weil brings out the same point in a powerful way in
her distinction between the natural and the supernatural God.
The desire to construct theodicies, for example, shows that a
philosopher lacks religious insight into the Christian approach to
evil. The philosopher sees religion as needing to justify God in
the face of evil, whereas the genuine religious response to evil
seeks a supernatural use for it.

The demise of philosophy as justification allows the possibility
of a less direct form of communication. Kierkegaard's indirect
communication of pseudonymous authorship and humour, for
example, fits in well with the Wittgensteinian picture of philosophy. Wittgenstein himself, after an almost complete lack of
examples in the *Tractatus*, uses examples as the major element of
his later philosophy. Examples are imperative in philosophy
because the role of philosophy is to analyse each context, each
language game, on its own terms.

Phillips, in particular, will always use examples rather than
generalizations in order to make a point, and will quote as fre-
quently from literature as from philosophy. Wittgenstein's own
writing exhibits a fine sense of humour also evident in Phillips;
indeed, Wittgenstein claimed that he could imagine a philosophy consisting entirely of jokes. These are not frivolous points:
rather, they reveal a major conflict between the Wittgensteinians
and the traditional philosophers of religion. For the latter, religious tenets, such as the existence of God, either should, or at
least can, be rationally justified or refuted. For the former, the
principle of rationality does not apply to the reality of God,
because God is such that philosophy can only comment accurately upon religious claims indirectly. Religion and philosophy
are grammatically disparate activities. In Wittgenstein's words,
'the symbolism of Christianity is wonderful beyond words, but

---

[32] Wittgenstein, *Culture and Value*, 16.

when people try to make a philosophical system out of it I find it disgusting'.[33]


### 3. THE INAPPROPRIATENESS OF THE PROOFS

We have seen, in the first section of this chapter, how Swinburne reinterprets the traditional Proofs into an inductive, cumulative probabilistic argument. It is utterly appropriate, for the tradition in which Swinburne stands, to use philosophy of religion as a discipline which can decide whether or not God exists. In sum, 'reason can reach a fairly well justified conclusion about the existence of God'.[34]

For the reasons given in this and the previous chapter, the Wittgensteinian school finds the Proofs a philosophically and religiously inappropriate reaction to the reality of God. Precursors to Wittgenstein, such as Luther and Kierkegaard, opposed the Proofs because they placed philosophical reasoning above religious faith, while Barth viewed even consideration of natural theology as a snare to tempt people away from the real intellectual task proper to religion, namely consideration of scripture.

In the Wittgensteinian school itself, two points in particular are made in favour of the inappropriateness of the Proofs. First, there is moral revulsion at the arrogance of philosophy that considers itself capable of judging God's existence and the kind of God who would actually be inferred by the Proofs. Wittgenstein himself wrote: 'It is a dogma of the Roman Catholic Church that the existence of God can be proved by natural reason. Now this dogma would make it impossible for me to be a Roman Catholic.'[35] This point is picked up by Rhees, for example, who considers the case of a man who knew nothing about God being told only about the God of the Proofs. Rhees asks: 'Would this give him any sense of the wonder and the glory of God? Would he not be justified if he answered, "What a horrible idea! Like a Frankenstein without limits, so that you cannot escape it. The most ghastly nightmare!"'[36]

[33] M. C. O'Drury, 'Some Notes on Conversations with Wittgenstein', in Rush Rhees, *Discussions of Wittgenstein*, 86.

[34] Swinburne, *The Existence of God*, 2.

[35] O'Drury, 'Conversations with Wittgenstein', 107–8.

[36] Rhees, *Without Answers*, 112.

Secondly, assuming that God can be proved or disproved shows a grammatical and logical misunderstanding of both language about God and the proper role of philosophy. The logic of the word 'God' entails that providing a rational foundation for the reality of God misconceives belief in God as a belief that can be grounded. The whole point of the Wittgensteinian school is that grounding is subsequent to taking certain things for granted; and one of these so-called groundless beliefs is belief in the existence of God. Malcolm writes for the whole tradition with these words:

> The obsessive concern with the proofs reveals the assumption that in order for religious belief to be intellectually respectable it *ought* to have a rational justification. *That* is the misunderstanding. It is like the idea that we are not justified in relying on memory until it has been proved reliable.[37]

None the less, the Wittgensteinian school does not find the Proofs worthless. If a Proof of God's existence is an attempt to find a rational justification of belief in God, then such a Proof is misconceived; but if a Proof is interpreted as an attempt to give glory to God by expressing his nature, then such a Proof is well conceived. The mistake now would be to see the Proofs as proofs at all; rather, they are best interpreted as expressions of faith.

For Wittgenstein himself, the Proofs are attempts of believers to show that there is no intellectual error in their 'belief' in God, not an attempt to bring anyone to faith by means of rational argument.[38] His followers have concentrated upon the grammatical religious insights contained in the Proofs: Malcolm, for example, argues in his famous essay on the ontological argument that Anselm's *Proslogion III* is making the grammatical point that God's reality is necessary. It is Phillips, however, who tries to express the non-philosophical import of the Proofs most fully.

For Phillips, it is important to treat the Proofs, not in their traditional inappropriate manner, but as efforts to give glory to God. The Proofs all contain religious insights which their formal structure can conceal. To deal with this formal structure as prior to the religious confession is the traditional philosophical mistake. 'So far from it being the formal proofs which give a rational

---

[37] Malcolm, 'The Groundlessness of Belief', 154–5.
[38] Wittgenstein, *Culture and Value*, 85.

foundation to the beliefs of the faithful, it was the lives of the faithful which breathed into the formal proofs whatever life they had.'[39]

Phillips deals explicitly with the three great traditional Proofs. He accepts that the Argument from Design was logically destroyed by the criticisms of Hume and Kant. Both philosophers, however, had respect for the argument, and Phillips suggests that their respect was for the religious expression behind the argument and not for its logical structure. The religious reaction was one of awe and wonder at the order and beauty in the world, and the Argument from Design was an attempt to give God the glory for this order and beauty. This reaction was in no way diminished by the collapse of the logic of the argument, a collapse heralded for Phillips as early as the book of Job. In Job we find a reference to the hippopotamus, which Phillips interprets as a comic comment upon the impossibility of rationalizing God's design:

It is meant to be a comic, ironic degradation of that form of rationalism which emanates in an argument to and from design. If we think we can understand God's creation in this way, bring it within the confines of human explanation, the challenging question is: What about the hippopotamus? What is its rationale in the scheme of things?[40]

The Cosmological Argument fails for similar reasons as the Teleological. It misconstrues God as a creator in the way that an all-powerful human being might be creator; in other words, it commits gross anthropomorphism with relation to God. Moreover, Hume showed conclusively how it is impossible to infer God from the world in any fashion at all. Any argument of an *a posteriori* kind can only be inconclusive—there are always other possible explanations of any of the phenomena of our experience—and so God is reduced to the status of an uncertain hypothesis.

None the less, the Cosmological Argument does have the merit of expressing the religious insight that God is other than this

[39] D. Z. Phillips, *Belief, Change and Forms of Life* (Basingstoke: Macmillan, 1986), 91.

[40] D. Z. Phillips, 'On Not Understanding God', unpublished paper delivered at the University of Birmingham, Oct. 1987, 22.

world and thus cannot be referred to in the way in which we refer to the world and its contents:

It might be said that the attempt of cosmological arguments to move from the fact that *anything* exists to the reality of God has within it the seeds of the religious beliefs we have been grappling with—namely, that it is in the existence of human beings and natural events *as such* that one comes to see what is meant by God's being other than the world.[41]

To say that God created the world is not, in Phillips's view, to put forward an explanatory hypothesis regarding how the world came into being: rather, it is to say that this world is God's world, and to see and partake of God's love for the world. It is also to see that to believe in God is to repudiate the way in which the world views things, because God is other than the world. The belief present in intellectual form in the Cosmological Argument is belief in God as the loving Creator of the world.[42]

It is easy to see how essentially religious insights became embodied in philosophical form. Before the rise of science, the heavens were seen as God's handiwork, and thus it is unsurprising that the intellectual religious response to this became the argument from design. It is equally unsurprising that the Cosmological Argument arose, coming at a time when the whole world could be seen as God's creation.

The Ontological Argument is also an example of a religious response to God wrongly cast in the form of a logical argument. Phillips writes of Anselm's combination of argument and praise that this is 'a mixture of what must essentially be kept apart; a mixture of philosophical grammatical observations and affirmations of faith'.[43] Since philosophy should be solely concerned with conceptual clarifications and grammatical observations, the Ontological Argument should not be seen as an attempt to show that there must be an instantiation of the concept of the being than which there can be no greater; rather, it is a believer's confession of faith or a philosopher's grammatical insight into the meaning of God.

Which of these two options is correct depends upon who is

---

[41] D. Z. Phillips, 'From World to God?', in *Faith and Philosophical Enquiry* (London: Routledge and Kegan Paul, 1970), 56–7.

[42] See Phillips, *Belief, Change and Forms of Life*, 91.

[43] D. Z. Phillips, *Religion without Explanation* (Oxford: Basil Blackwell, 1976), 179.

saying that there is (or is not) a God. If it is a believer or non-believer, then it is a confession; but

in so far as these words come from the mouths of philosophers discussing the logical status of belief in God, the most that Anselm's arguments can show is that both statements about God are confused if the notion involved is contingent existence. The same confusion exists in these remarks . . . whether they be expressed by believers or atheists respectively.[44]

Phillips echoes Malcolm's interpretation of Anselm's argument, that it shows the grammatical mistake of treating God as a being who might or might not exist. Philosophers can agree upon this philosophical observation without this entailing anything about whether or not they do believe in God's reality.

Although the Proofs as philosophical arguments fail, and are inappropriate, this does not mean that the religious responses behind the Proofs are irrational. The meaning of rationality is different in different contexts, and it does not follow that if one cannot give a philosophically rational justification of a belief that the belief in question is irrational. No such justification is available for a belief in the goodness of generosity, but this does not mean that therefore this belief is irrational.

Thus Phillips reinterprets the Proofs as expressions of faith or grammatical insight, and not as deductive or inductive arguments. We can see from these two chapters that to decide whether or not Phillips is right to do this, or whether Swinburne is correct that the Proofs are appropriate as philosophical justifications, requires a decision about the correctness of the cognitive, expressibility, and rationality principles, and the whole areas of religious language, the concept of God, and the proper role of philosophy to which they correspond. It is to considerations of the particular criticisms in these areas of traditional philosophy of religion against Phillips, and Phillips's replies to traditional philosophy of religion, that I now turn.

[44] Ibid. 177.

# 3

# The Depth Of Disagreement

---

In this chapter, I will discuss how several representative cognitive philosophers of religion criticize Phillips in three basic areas. First, the cognitive principle entails that what believers mean by religious language is what cognitive philosophers have taken it to mean. Phillips is accused of being a non-cognitivist and revisionist, of having misunderstood what believers actually take language about God to mean.

Secondly, the expressibility principle entails a particular type of definition of God. Phillips is accused of being an atheist for rejecting the standard philosophy of religion definition of God and the possibility of any definition of God whatever.

Thirdly, the rationality principle entails that belief in God is open to justification, and Phillips is accused of cutting belief in God off from any genuine criticism by denying this and adopting the idea of language games.

I will deal with these three criticisms and Phillips's replies to them in the first three sections. I shall argue that, both for traditional philosophy of religion and for Phillips's Wittgensteinianism, the depth of these disagreements is so great that no solution appears possible. In Section 4 I shall show that this point is occasionally hinted at in some of Phillips's writings, but that he does not seem to go far enough in accepting it. My conclusion is that to understand the dispute between the traditional philosophical attitude to the Proofs and the Wittgensteinian challenge to this, we need to reach more deeply than the protagonists themselves have realized.

## 1. PHILLIPS AS REVISIONIST

The argument that Phillips's account is plainly inaccurate when it comes to how believers have actually used religious language is found in many of the cognitive philosophers of religion. Swinburne, for example, argues that a survey of what religious believers had taken their words to mean would show that Phillips's account was clearly wrong.[1] He argues that Phillips's account of prayer, for example, is 'a totally false account of the meaning of the prayers of most who have prayed in the Christian and other theistic traditions over many centuries, including the present century'.[2] Hick also claims that Phillips's Wittgensteinian portrayal of religious language is revisionary rather than descriptive,[3] adding that his portrayal is not 'an objective analysis of the language of faith as living speech but is instead recommending a quite new use for it'.[4]

The various cognitive descriptions of God outlined in the first chapter are not intended by traditional philosophers of religion as a comment upon the meaning which religious language should have; rather, they are intended to be accurate reflections of the standard way in which Christians have used their words about God. God is a being claimed to exist independently of us, and it is a factual issue whether or not such a being does exist. Hick writes that it is 'presupposed in the christian [*sic*] scriptures, creeds, confessions, prayers, sermons and theologies that it is a factual truth that God exists'.[5]

One of Phillips's replies to this, as we have seen, is that to talk of God existing is to impose the alien grammar of contingency upon God. Hick replies that even if we talk of God as necessarily existent, as Phillips suggests that we do, it is still a factual issue whether or not there is such a being.[6]

For Phillips, this is to misconstrue the nature of grammatically unconfused belief and disbelief. Genuine atheism is an admission that the language of religion means nothing to one; just as religious belief of a genuine kind is a total endorsement of the primary elements of religious language. It is a grammatical precondition of religious belief that, for oneself, God is real. Phillips writes that 'the idea of God is such that the possibility of the non-existence of God is logically precluded'.[7] To have doubts about

---

[1] Swinburne, *The Coherence of Theism*, 92–3.
[2] Swinburne, *Faith and Reason*, 140–1 n.
[3] Hick, *Philosophy of Religion*, 92–3.
[4] Hick, *God and the Universe of Faiths*, 8.     [5] Ibid. 25.
[6] Ibid. 29.     [7] Phillips, *The Concept of Prayer*, 14.

God's reality is to have doubts about the form of life of which religion is a part, and the intelligibility of the language one uses in such a context. The only reason for the issue of the reality of God to arise in a religious context is when confronted by the claims of other religions in favour of the reality of their God; and this is a conflict of ways of life, not a clash of factual hypotheses.

The same comments apply to the notion that God has an existence independently of us. To talk of God in such a way is to talk of a natural God, a God who is like us in that he has a determinate existence. But this kind of talk misconstrues the real nature of belief in God:

Coming to see that there is a God is not like coming to see that an additional being exists. If it were, there would be an extension of one's knowledge of facts, but no extension of one's understanding. Coming to see that there is a God involves seeing a new meaning in one's life, and being given a new understanding.[8]

One's life changing in such a way cannot be the cause of a discovery of a new fact; for there is no independent God, no 'new fact', to be discovered. Rather, coming to believe in God is to see what is already here in a completely new light.

There is equally no sense in the view that God's existence is not factual. If we agree that the language of being happy does not apply to my desk, this does not mean that the language of being unhappy does. The whole point is that the language of facts does not apply to God:

In saying that something either is or is not a fact, I am not describing the something in question. To say that x is a fact is to say something about the grammar of x; it is to indicate what it would and would not be sensible to say or do in connection with it. To say that the concept of divine reality does not share this grammar is to reject the possibility of talking about God in the way in which one talks about matters of fact.[9]

Another reason for this is that in the case of the reality of God, it is not obviously clear how one could resolve whether or not God is real. However, in a question of fact it is clear what kind

[8] Phillips, 'Faith, Scepticism and Religious Understanding', in *Faith and Philosophical Enquiry*, 17.
[9] Phillips, 'Philosophy, Theology and the Reality of God', in *Faith and Philosophical Enquiry*, 2–3.

of dispute is concerned. If you say 'There is a tree', and I say 'No, there's nothing there', it is obvious in what way we would try to resolve the dispute. We would go to the supposed object and try to touch it; perhaps if the day was foggy we would come back to look when the fog had cleared. The same basic principle applies to more subtle cases such as the existence of electrons: there are certain experiments designed to demonstrate whether or not electrons exist. It is the mistake of seeing the issue of God's reality as having an equally easy or agreed upon method of resolution that has misled traditional philosophers of religion into seeing religious language as cognitive.

The objection that he is a revisionist is one that Phillips has tried to refute by showing that, although his account of religious language does not allow God's independent existence or factuality, these elements are not parts of the way in which religious believers actually use their language in any case. Nevertheless, Phillips is not simply taking part in a survey of what religious believers have said. He argues that it is a mistake to look at what believers say about their beliefs, and take their reflection to constitute the belief. A man or woman will pray, and know what they are doing when praying, but may then be unable to give a reflective account of what they were doing while in prayer. Phillips argues that philosophers should not want 'a Gallup poll on people's views about religion', but should look at the beliefs and prayers in their worshipful context.[10]

Once one does look at the contexts in which religious language is used, it becomes obvious, in Phillips's view, that there is much diversity of belief and accounts of belief. It is not only believers who vary in their accounts: 'the philosophers vary in their accounts of religious beliefs as much as the believers themselves'.[11] When dealing with such accounts, we must pursue our grammatical analysis in the face of inaccurate description on the part of some believers. For example, '*the same* believers who say that the existence of God is a fact would, if pressed, admit that the existence of God is not like the discovery of a matter of fact, and that there is no question of God ceasing to exist, of having

[10] Phillips, *The Concept of Prayer*, 1–3.
[11] Phillips (ed.), *Religion and Understanding*, Introduction, p. 3.

existed for a certain length of time, or of having come into existence'.[12] We can only, in pursuing philosophical clarification, take an example of a believer and delve beneath his account of religion to the role which his beliefs play in his life and the way in which they come out in directly religious language. This is to investigate the depth grammar of religious language, its meaning in its proper context of worship, rather than the surface grammar of 'God exists' where 'God exists' appears to be of the form 'a particular fact is the case'.

It is my contention that the disagreement between Phillips and his critics here runs very deep. Superficially it looks as if their debate is resolvable by an examination of what believers say in and about their beliefs. Yet the issue is clearly not as simple as this. Phillips, like Wittgenstein, is keen to use examples; and his examples do show that there are people who believe in the way Phillips describes. He uses examples from literature and from his own and others' experience to support his claim. We have seen how he stands within a tradition of philosophy of religion which has consistently repudiated what is described in current thinking as cognitive religious language.

Equally, Phillips admits that there are people who have believed in the way that Hick and his other critics have described.[13] The issue now becomes whether Phillips or his critics is giving a more accurate account of religious belief. The 'accuracy', in this case, refers to the historically dominant form of Christianity (since both Phillips and most of his critics are concerned about this one religion almost exclusively). The cognitive charge against him says that Phillips has misconstrued what believers have held about their Christian beliefs throughout history, and in the present day.[14] According to the cognitivist principle, Phillips is a revisionist.

This, I think, is an impossible charge to substantiate. The

[12] Phillips, 'Religious Belief and Philosophical Enquiry', in *Faith and Philosophical Enquiry*, 71.

[13] D. Z. Phillips, 'Religion and Epistemology: Some Contemporary Confusions', in *Faith and Philosophical Enquiry*, 127.

[14] Note that historical dominance is not for Phillips a good criterion of what is to count as a truly religious perspective. Unconfused language games can die out; confused ones can live on. See *Belief, Change and Forms of Life*, 97–103.

difficulty is that the word 'God' is used 'in a bewildering variety of ways',[15] to use H. P. Owen's phrase. Detailed discussions of the meaning of God often come up with a large variety of meanings, even within Christianity: thus Ward writes that 'it is not entirely clear what it means to believe in God',[16] while Macquarrie contends that 'innumerable meanings have at one time or another been given to the word "God" or its equivalents'.[17]

Macquarrie makes a useful and interesting distinction between religious theism and philosophical theism. The former entails the reality of a personal and transcendent God. It is the standard Jewish conception, for example, concentrating on revelation, action, and worship. The latter depersonalizes God and begins to search for reasons for and against God's existence. It is found initially in the meeting of Jewish and Greek thought, and emphasizes rationality and reflection.

The idea that Christianity is an amalgam of two very different traditions, the Jewish and the Greek, is a common one. The former can be seen to coincide more with the Wittgensteinian conception of God, and the latter more with the cognitivists'. One stresses mystery, the other stresses rationality, as Leszek Kolakowski points out:

The enemies of philosophy in the Christian world argued that to employ human reason and human logic in trying to fathom the divine mysteries amounted to a godless hubris, we ought to be satisfied, in humility, with the simple language of Scripture and not exercise our curiosity in a vain philosophising which is pagan by definition. Philosophers replied that our Reason is God's gift, and limited though it may be, it can—if modest and enlightened by faith, according to some, or even without this restriction, according to others—contribute greatly to our understanding of the marvellous divine governorship of the universe.[18]

In short, then, there are major strands within Christianity which seem more suited to Phillips's account of religious belief than to that of his critics. The mystical tradition, including figures such as St John of the Cross and Meister Eckhart, is certainly not to do

[15] H. P. Owen, *Concepts of Deity* (London and Basingstoke: Macmillan, 1971), p. vii.

[16] Keith Ward, *The Concept of God* (Oxford: Basil Blackwell, 1974), 3.

[17] Macquarrie, *In Search of Deity*, 14.

[18] Leszek Kolakowski, 'The Worshippers' God and the Philosophers' God', *TLS* (23 May 1986), 257.

with God's factual existence. The Reformation, Quakerism, and Barthianism all have more affinities with Phillips than with the cognitivists. This is not to deny that there are strands within historical Christianity that fit in with the accounts of cognitivists: examples include Catholicism generally, some conservative Protestantism, and those influenced by nineteenth-century idealism. Phillips is concerned with the retention of mystery far more than with the excessively strained use of reason. His account of the distinction between his kind of philosophy and that of his critics is similar to the distinction Kolakowski made:

The great divide in contemporary philosophy of religion, is not between those who offer religious explanations, and those who offer non-religious explanations, of the limits of human existence, but between those who recognise and those who do not recognise, that the limits of human existence are beyond human understanding.[19]

Phillips's point is that religion accepts what is beyond understanding; and that the philosophy which his critics offer entails that everything can be understood. Historically, it can be said that Phillips follows the strand of emphasizing mystery in religion, while his critics follow the strand that emphasizes rational understanding. While Swinburne emphasizes factual uses of religious language, Phillips emphasizes the non-factual. It is clear, however, that the distinction between Jewish and Greek thought plays upon polarized extremes. Cognitivists do not always intend to depersonalize God; Phillips does not intend to return to what Weil called the 'natural' God of the Old Testament. The point is that the variety of meanings of God within Christianity, and the historical support for Phillips's conception, overcome the simple charge that Phillips is a revisionist; for there is no single dominant conception of God, even within Christianity, to be revised. Macquarrie prefers the notion of dialectical theism to any alternative; but it is noteworthy that this is not a description of a historically dominant form of belief, but a *recommendation* of what Christianity should be. I now turn to the objection that Phillips is commending a conception of God which is quite opposed to any proper Christian understanding of the divine.

---

[19] Phillips, 'On Not Understanding God', 1.

## 2. PHILLIPS AS ATHEIST

The debate here goes deeper than a mere historical divergence of emphasis. For implicit in much of the writing against Phillips, and explicit in some of it, is the claim that Phillips is not only wrong to see religion as he does, but that his views entail atheism. In other words, Phillips has not only misunderstood the historically dominant form of Christianity, he has also failed to see the essential elements of Christian belief which make it what it is. Hick, for example, claims that atheism is the denial that there is an extra consciousness called God, and that Phillips endorses such a denial. Hick's actual words are these:

I take it that he [Phillips] denies the existence of an all-powerful and limitlessly loving God. I take it, that is, that he denies that in addition to all the many human consciousnesses there is another consciousness which is the consciousness of God, and that this God is the creator of the universe and is both all-powerful and limitlessly loving.[20]

Phillips rejects this, and I think quite rightly. All that Hick is saying is that Phillips rejects what the existence of God means as far as Hick is concerned. To say that God is an additional consciousness to ours is 'a philosopher's gloss on the nature of religious belief'.[21] This is quite correct. Hick has assumed that religious belief entails that God is an extra consciousness; but this assumption would rule out many kinds of belief that are commonly known as religions (such as mystical traditions, some Eastern sects). It would take further argument to show that religious belief *should* entail that God is an extra consciousness. The difference here, then, is that Hick and Phillips are working with different conceptions of God: and this is a much deeper disagreement than Hick's charge of atheism allows. Phillips is intent, not on rejecting the reality of God, but on rejecting the traditional definition of God given by philosophy of religion.

A similar kind of objection to Phillips is that he makes religious language purely expressive. Mackie, for example, argues that praise requires an existing object that is the subject of praise, or else it is purely an expression of one's own feelings. Either

[20] John Hick, 'Remarks', in Stuart C. Brown (ed.), *Reason and Religion* (London: Cornell University Press, 1977), 122.

[21] Phillips, *Belief, Change and Forms of Life*, 73.

God is believed to be real, for Mackie, or else he is not and all religious language is an atheistic expression of one's attitude to life. Phillips, he thinks, holds the latter view.[22] Either God exists independently of us, or he is a thought in our minds.

Phillips reacts by pointing out the paucity and inaccuracy of the dichotomy presented to him. He argues that an analysis of the depth grammar of religious language reveals that, for a believer, God is neither an independent consciousness nor a human thought.[23] To present us with only these two options is to impose upon the religious language game an alien grammar, and hence an alien dichotomy. Not only is this dichotomy an inappropriate one, but an analysis of religious language being used in worshipful contexts shows that it is 'woefully impoverished'.[24] Phillips admits that religious language is partly expressive,[25] but his point is that this does not mean that God does not exist, but simply that he does not exist in the way his critics suppose. To say that religious language is expressive is not to imply that there is no more to religion than a linguistic component:

It is an elementary mistake to think that because the meaning of prayer is to be found by referring to the institution of religion or religious language, what the prayer *says* must be something about language or an institution; about 'mere words' as it is sometimes put. We use language when we pray, but we do not pray to language![26]

For Phillips, these rejections of his critics are based upon grammatical analysis of religious beliefs in their contexts. The difficulty here is that while Phillips is analysing one strand of tradition, his opponents seem to be analysing another. To make a further claim that his opponents are wrong to do this is problematic; and, as we shall see later, Phillips does retreat from doing this on occasions. One situation in which he seems to go through with his criticism, however, is against what I have called the expressibility principle.

---

[22] Mackie, *The Miracle of Theism*, 225–7.

[23] Phillips, *Belief, Change and Forms of Life*, 74.

[24] Phillips, 'The Friends of Cleanthes', 100–1.

[25] D. Z. Phillips, 'Seeking the Poem in the Rain: Order and Contingency in the Poetry of R. S. Thomas', in *Through A Darkening Glass: Philosophy, Literature and Cultural Change* (Oxford: Basic Blackwell, 1982), 177–9.

[26] Phillips, *The Concept of Prayer*, 57.

It is not only the case for Phillips that the God of the type defined by Swinburne is a purely natural, philosophical being, an existent among existents, nor is it only the case that traditional philosophers of religion have equated such a God with the God of religion; for example, Phillips writes of Mackie that 'he equates philosophical theism with religious belief. He refuses to call anything else an example of religion.'[27] More than this, Phillips repudiates the very idea of a definition of God. A proper understanding of the mystery of God, that we only understand God when we realize that we cannot understand him, shows that any definition of God is misconceived. We gain our idea of what God means by worshipping him or observing others worshipping; but we show our misunderstanding if we try to convert that idea into a definition. The rules of the religious language game do not allow for any other method of defining God.

I wish to elucidate here the level on which these disagreements between Phillips and his critics lie. The critics refuse to countenance Phillips's account of religious belief as either historically accurate or as an acceptable revision, because it is equivalent to atheism. This position depends upon accepting their view of the nature of God, and the ways in which we would go about confirming that God exists. Phillips, on the other hand, rejects his critics' view of religion as historically inaccurate and grammatically incorrect. This position depends upon acceptance of Phillips's own idea of what constitutes religion and the ways in which we can ascertain this.

I have argued that, on the historical issue, while Phillips espouses a strand of religion which emphasizes mystery, rawness, and impersonality, his critics prefer the strand which emphasizes comprehensibility, rationality, and personality. Each strand has a long basis in history, so any historical survey would neither fully support nor refute these two accounts. Thus we move on to the normative level of what religion should consist in, and again there is fundamental disagreement here. This appears to be as unresolvable as the historical issue. If one only encounters the writings of cognitive philosophers of religion, or only the writings of Wittgenstein, the issue would seem very clear cut. Yet once one is aware of both sets of thought, the possibility of

---

[27] Phillips, 'The Friends of Cleanthes', 94.

a resolution seems remote. There is simply too great a diversity amongst religious believers to be able to assert one historically dominant strand against the others. Equally, there are simply too many different conceptions of what constitutes the normative essence of Christianity, and the ways in which we could decide which conception is correct, for us to expect the simple charges of revisionist and atheist made against Phillips to stand, or to expect Phillips's grammatical analysis, which results in the rejection of the cognitive and expressibility principles, to be obviously correct. The issue here appears to need a detailed discussion of how one should make judgements between normative claims, and it needs this before we can judge whether Swinburne or Phillips has a proper conception of God and the meaning of religious language.

The worry is that such a discussion will produce no definite results. Swinburne's normative conception of religion comes from his historical and philosophical certainty that belief in God is cognitive, that God can be defined, and that God should be defined in the way in which he does. These are certainties which pervade traditional philosophy of religion. Hick, for example, who has much awareness of other religions, and who is a confirmed pluralist, finds philosophical reasons for moving away from what he sees as the traditional exclusivist Christian conception of God to a Kantian distinction between the real (noumenal) God and the apparent (phenomenal) God.[28] Yet, if one does not share Hick's philosophical basis, as Wittgensteinians clearly do not, there is no reason for starting in this direction at all. The problems here are in trying to decide which direction is the correct one, and, more fundamentally, whether there is any meaningful sense to the notion of a right direction at such a fundamental level.

Phillips rejects the cognitive norm of religion and philosophy, as the cognitivists reject his. My point is that the normative conceptions that each philosophical school has are so deep that one needs to accept or reject certain fundamental principles or beliefs prior to one's acceptance of the right normative conception of God. Thus we are back to seeing that this debate about the appropriateness of the Proofs cannot be resolved without an

---

[28] Hick, *An Interpretation of Religion*, 236–49.

acceptance or rejection of the most fundamental elements of two major philosophical schools.

The nature of this problem can perhaps be made clearer by an example. You and I are interested in who is the best male tennis player in the world. I argue that the player who shows the best form over the entire year is the best player: he has shown the greatest stamina, the greatest consistency, and has won the most tournaments. (This is in fact how the number one tennis player on the computer ranking is worked out.) You argue that the four Grand Slam tournaments, the greatest tennis events, should provide the main criterion. If a player wins three or four of them in a year, or is the only player to appear in all four finals, then he is the number one player: the football World Cup, for example, is intentionally about teams being able to rise to the big occasion, not about the play of the previous four years.

The point is that in this situation stalemate seems to have been reached. Two different sets of criteria are being used in making a judgement, and there is no neutral standpoint from which to assess these criteria. The criteria precede our making of judgements; unless one of the criteria is given up, no agreement can be possible. If consistency over the year makes the best player, then we have a different number one tennis player from the one we would have if performance in the Grand Slams were what counted. The difficulty is in seeing how one can judge whether one of these criteria is the right one.

The situation between the cognitivists and the Wittgensteinians is similar to this. If the cognitivists' criteria for assessing what is to count as an atheist are accepted—someone who rejects the possibility of defining God in general and their definition in particular—then Phillips is an atheist. Yet if Phillips's criteria are accepted—that grammatical observation of actual religious language shows that there should be no definition of God—then the cognitivists are clearly not discussing God at all. The most interesting issue here, to be discussed later in the book, is whether a definitive assessment of these criteria is possible to avoid an apparent stalemate.

## 3. PHILLIPS AS OBSTRUCTIONIST

The other common objection to Phillips's position is that his taking over of the language game theory makes religious belief immune from external criticism, such as philosophical reason. Kenny has this in mind when he writes:

Unfortunately, Wittgenstein's influence on the philosophy of religion has been disastrous. . . . The concept of language-game is an obscure and ambiguous one in Wittgenstein's own writings; in the hands of some of his admirers it has become a stone-wall defence against any demand for a justification of belief in God.[29]

The force behind this criticism is that the language game theory makes religion autonomous. Hick concludes from this that there can be no reasons in favour of or against taking up the religious language game. If it cannot be verified or falsified, then there are no grounds for or against the claims of religious belief. 'The most distinctive feature of this view is that religious language is autonomous, so that statements made within it are invulnerable to external criticism.'[30]

This criticism is quite mistaken. The critics of Phillips's position have taken the 'ambiguous' language game theory and decided that it unambiguously entails that religious language is autonomous. Yet any reading of Phillips's work will show how concerned he is to stress the links between religion and other forms of life. If these links were not there, then religion would not have the force it does for so many people. Remarking on his intention in the *Concept Of Prayer*, he writes that, 'so far from denying the connections between prayer and these features of human life, I argued that if such connections are severed, the religious significance of the "prayer" becomes problematic'.[31]

Language games are not completely separate realms of linguistic activity; rather, they are interconnected so that the words of one language game can and do affect words of another. Philosophy does have an effect upon religious language, for the ideas of philosophers can permeate down through intellectual discussion into the worshipful life. (For example, doubts about the factual accuracy of the Virgin Birth expressed by David Jenkins, Don Cupitt, and others has certainly had an effect upon primary religious language.) If 'God is real' was completely separate in

---

[29] Kenny, 'In Defence of God', 145.

[30] John Hick, 'Sceptics and Believers', in John Hick (ed.), *Faith and the Philosophers* (London: Macmillan, 1964), 238.

[31] Phillips, *Belief, Change and Forms of Life*, 9.

meaning from 'this table is real', then there would be no reason to use the same word 'real' in each context.

The notion of family resemblances, discussed in Chapter 1, shows how different language games are connected. A black hole and a man hole are very different; but if we know what each phrase means, we can see why 'hole' is the appropriate word in each case. The key is only to describe a language game in the right way, since ultimately no language game has any justification at all, rational or otherwise. Unless we are participants in a language game, the notion of rational justification makes no sense. We must take for granted the fundamental precepts of a language game or else we would be unable to play that language game and to use that language. There is nothing unique about the religious language game here: it is not alone in having a basic structure which one accepts if one is playing that game, and which one cannot reject as being unjustified because the whole notion of justification makes no sense at this fundamental level.

The cognitive criticism is that Phillips's account does not allow God's existence to be justified or even to be susceptible of justification. The famous challenge of Antony Flew to philosophers to provide circumstances in which one could say that God's existence had been falsified, and the taking up of that challenge by the philosophers addressed, typifies the stance of Phillips's critics.[32] Statements about God are indicative, and are therefore open to verification and falsification.[33] Kenny makes the even stronger claim that justification is essential to religious belief: 'To me it seems that if belief in the existence of God cannot be rationally justified, there can be no good reasons for adopting any of the traditional monotheistic religions.'[34] This may be true for a particular kind of religious belief, perhaps the kind of Catholic belief which Kenny was brought up with; but it is a misconception to suppose that in every kind of religious belief acceptance

---

[32] Antony Flew *et al.*, 'Theology and Falsification', in Antony Flew and Alasdair Macintyre (eds.), *New Essays in Philosophical Theology* (London: SCM Press, 1955). R. M. Hare appears to be a non-cognitivist with his conception of 'blik'; he does think that Flew is entirely successful on his own grounds.

[33] John Hick, 'The Justification of Religious Belief', *Theology*, lxxxi (Mar. 1968), 102. See Mackie, *The Miracle of Theism*, 228.

[34] Anthony Kenny, *The Five Ways* (London: Routledge and Kegan Paul, 1969), 4.

of the power of (philosophical) justification should lie deeper than belief in God. The rationality principle reduces all kinds of religious belief to one.

Equally, however, the kind of religion which the Wittgensteinians describe is a particular kind. Phillips asserts explicitly against Kenny[35] and Hick[36] that the attempt to provide a rational justification—or, indeed, any justification at all—of religious belief misconstrues the nature of religion. Within religion, one's form of life gives rise to the language one uses; therefore, it is quite illegitimate to take an alien form of language, such as 'justification', and attempt to apply it to the religious form of life.

Again it must be seen that Phillips's point has limited application. To the kind of religion he is describing, it is quite correct to say that justification has no place. However, to the more rationalistic kind of religion, justification is quite in order. Phillips is simply doing what his critics are doing: rejecting one of these kinds of talk as not counting as religious.

This can be brought out in Phillips's discussion of his critics' use of 'reality'. Mackie affirms that in discussions of religious language, we must employ our criteria from ordinary language,[37] while Hick claims that to gain any meaning for 'real', we need a paradigm case of the use of the word, and this is provided by the case of our ordinary senses' perception of 'real'.[38] Phillips retorts, following Wittgenstein, that language is too complex and diverse to exhibit any neutral paradigm cases of real.[39] He writes that 'the distinction between the real and the unreal does not come to the same thing in every context. To think otherwise is to fall into a deep confusion about the relation between language and reality.'[40] The confusion is to suppose that we somehow have a notion of reality prior to language. Phillips's point is that it is our participation in a language game that gives rise to our notions of reality; hence the adoption of a notion of reality that applies to *all* language is grammatically misguided.

Despite the force of this point, it can still be said that some religions or strands of religion do have a conception of reality as

---

[35] Phillips, *Belief, Change and Forms of Life*, 4.     [36] Ibid. 33.
[37] Mackie, *The Miracle of Theism*, 224–5.
[38] Hick, *Philosophy of Religion*, 58–9.
[39] Phillips (ed.), *Religion and Understanding*, 4.
[40] D. Z. Phillips, 'Religious Belief and Philosophical Enquiry', 63.

described by Phillips's critics. Phillips is right that for some religious strands, reality is the way he describes it; but to say that all religious strands are that way is to fall into the universalizing of one way of using a term that he accuses his critics of.

This is also true of the disagreement over how statements in language gain their truth and falsity. For more traditional philosophers, as we have seen, language gets its meaning from correspondence to external reality. Phillips is right that not all religious believers would accept this account: not only the philosophers and theologians whom we have seen to be sympathetic to Phillips's approach, but also many sects and many individuals do not see God as an external, independent consciousness. The problem is that equally many believers and many thinkers have taken God to be an external reality, and thus the debate is the now familiar one of a comparatively superficial disagreement leading to a fundamental divergence over such basic topics as the concept of God and the way in which language gets its meaning.

The same is true of the task of philosophy of religion. We have seen that this task is one of rational justification or refutation of belief in the existence of God for traditional philosophy of religion. Phillips argues in response to this that:

in no other branch of philosophy is it assumed so widely that the purpose of the investigation is to establish the truth or falsity of particular existential claims. For example, we do not say that philosophy establishes whether tables and chairs exist, but many do say that philosophy establishes that God does not exist.[41]

His point is that in other areas of philosophy, we do not look for justifications of the existence of the subject of that field. It is a mistake to assume that suddenly, in the philosophy of religion, this should alter.

The traditional objection to this response is that, in the case of chairs and tables, no one really has any doubt about their existence; but in the case of God there is considerable disagreement about his existence. Therefore it is the philosopher's business to discover whether or not God exists. Phillips has a reply here too. He argues that a grammatical study of religious belief shows that for a believer God's existence is unquestionable, just as the

---

[41] Phillips, *Religion without Explanation*, 152.

existence of the physical world is unquestionable for everyone but the most sceptical. It is therefore a grammatical mistake to foist attempted justifications on to a part of a language game in which justification plays no role.

For the cognitivists, the rationality principle holds good. For Phillips, however, philosophy does not give us a new perspective on something, but reminds us of what we already know. Philosophy's task is simply the untying of knots caused by conceptual confusion.[42] It is neither for nor against religion, since the validity of a religion is only properly questioned within a conceptually clear understanding of religious belief. Philosophy provides some understanding, not a justification, of religious discourse.[43] Phillips's attitude to philosophy is summed up in his assertion that, even in the face of current philosophical appeals for justification, 'the task of philosophy remains unchanged: as always, it has to endeavour to understand what lies before it'.[44]

Again, the disagreement between Phillips and his critics is a normative one. It could not be decided by reference to what philosophers have done; for clearly some philosophical traditions have written in each of the ways Phillips and his critics describe. (One thinks of Wittgenstein, of course, and also of some phenomenology and existentialist philosophy in the case of Phillips, and the empiricist and rationalist traditions in the case of his critics.) The question now becomes in what way we should philosophize, and what is actually involved in asking such a question.

To answer this in favour of either school in this debate is to accept the truth or falsity of the fundamental principles I have discussed. However, because these principles are so fundamental, and are of the nature of positions from which to argue rather than steps in an argument, it is extremely difficult to see how one can make a decision about the principles themselves. Moreover, I have argued that one's attitude to the appropriateness of the Proofs depends upon one's reactions to these principles; hence the apparent impossibility of a judgement of general acceptability upon whether or not the Proofs are appropriate.

---

[42] Phillips, *Belief, Change and Forms of Life*, 118–19.
[43] Phillips, *The Concept of Prayer*, 24.
[44] Phillips, *Belief, Change and Forms of Life*, p. xi.

Neither the tacit cognitivist assumption that reason can over-come this situation, nor the Wittgensteinian assumption that belief in God is groundless, provides neutrally cogent responses.

Whenever this kind of conclusion is reached, the fact of relat-ivity—the presence of a diversity of possibly correct positions—must be considered. Phillips has been taken as flirting with acceptance of such a fact,[45] and I shall discuss his writings on the subject in the next section. The diversity of viewpoints about the appropriateness of the Proofs, and about the presuppositions underlying the debate, is a fact that cannot be denied by either Swinburne or Phillips, since the very differences between them are a clear indication of the fact.

In the face of relativity, Phillips seems to be caught upon the horns of a dilemma. On the one hand he wishes to assert the diversity of religious and philosophical points of view, and yet on the other he wishes to hold a genuine distinction between true religion and superstition in the face of diversity. It is this dilemma which I shall now discuss.

## 4. PHILLIPS AS RELATIVIST

Phillips has two measures which, I contend, take him in his own view beyond the limitations of the fact of relativity. These are grammatical clarification and 'knowing when to stop'. The former is the proper philosophical task which can show up beliefs for what they are; in the example of theodicies, we find the gram-matically unacceptable position of God, who is good, being morally contemptible, because approving of evil. The latter is the point at which notions of right and wrong cease to have any meaning; there is no issue of whether playing this language game or that one is the right thing, hence language games and forms of life are not right or wrong, and are not subject to relativity. I shall discuss this latter point in some detail in Chapter 6.

Phillips wholeheartedly accepts the point that religion means different things to different people. Not only are there the very obvious differences between beliefs of different religions, but also

---

[45] Gareth Moore, 'Review of *Faith after Foundationalism*', *New Blackfriars*, 71 (Mar. 1990), 151–4.

there is much diversity of belief within a single religion. Even within a single congregation it would be impossible to find two people with exactly the same religious beliefs. This is clear to Phillips. 'When one considers the different ways in which religious believers react to birth, death, bereavement, good fortune, or disaster, one has to conclude that religion means very different things to different people.'[46] Philosophical accounts of religion are as diverse as the religious beliefs which they describe. Not only is their subject matter diverse, but the characters and experiences of the philosophers will be diverse too:

What a philosopher says about religion may show how much religion means to him, or whether, for him, it means anything at all. Once this is recognised one can see why philosophical accounts of religion will always be different; they do not possess the same insights or the same beliefs.[47]

Thus, philosophical activity cannot be divorced from the person of the philosopher. This is also true, of course, of Phillips's own prescribed philosophical task of grammatical analysis. This task will never produce one single definitive conclusion. 'It ought to be clear how superficial it is to regard conceptual analysis as some kind of philosophical technique cut off from religious insights we may or may not possess.'[48]

This does not mean, however, that the difference between true religion and superstition is a purely subjective one. A religious belief is superstitious if it is grammatically misconceived or morally bankrupt. For example, to say of the God of Christianity that he condones gratuitous murder would be to show a misunderstanding of the loving nature of God. Phillips rejects the Old Testament conception of God as commanding his chosen people to slaughter other nations: this is a grammatically and morally unacceptable belief in God. He also concurs with Simone Weil in her reasons for rejecting the conception of God of the Athenians who massacred the inhabitants of Melos:

How can one prove that this idea of God is wrong? Simone Weil answers as follows: 'The first proof that they were in the wrong lies in the fact that, contrary to their assertion, it happens, though extremely rarely, that a man will forbear out of pure generosity to command where

---

[46] Phillips, *Religion and Understanding*, 5.    [47] Ibid.    [48] Ibid. 3.

he has the power to do so. That which is possible for man is also possible for God.'

In this answer, Simone Weil is profoundly right. What other proof of a religion could one ever ask for or hope to possess?[49]

We have already seen that the cognitivist philosophers of religion do not answer this question in the way in which Phillips thinks correct. None the less, Phillips's point is clear. To ascribe to the God that one believes in a lower morality than that of the best human being is to fail to understand what is meant by God. Belief in an adequate conception of God must itself be morally praiseworthy: to imagine that one's religion is better than another's is arrogant intolerance, and therefore must be superstition rather than true religion. It is to imagine that one is better off than someone else because one has something the other person does not have, and this belief, since it puts oneself in a superior position, is immoral and therefore superstitious.

We know that God's will is good; therefore any bad purpose cannot be God's. The belief of the Yorkshire Ripper, that God told him to kill, can be ruled out as genuine religious belief, because it ascribes a bad purpose to God.

The difference between true religion and superstition can also be seen in less extreme examples. For instance, Phillips writes of three mothers' reactions to their handicapped children. The first mother says that 'only my religious faith keeps me going. Of one thing I am sure: my child's place in heaven is secure.'[50] Phillips's response to this is to write: 'I do not find it impressive religiously. Indeed, I should want to go further and say that it has little to do with religion, being much closer to superstition.'[51] We find what Phillips means when he turns to the other two mothers. He says that they show a religious reaction to having mentally handicapped children; because 'both mothers refuse to look upon belief in God as an explanatory hypothesis'.[52]

One of these mothers, when asked why it had happened to her to have a mentally handicapped child, answered, 'Why shouldn't

[49] Phillips, 'On the Christian Conception of God', in *Faith and Philosophical Enquiry*, 248. He quotes Simone Weil, *Waiting on God*, trans. Emma Craufurd (London: Routledge and Kegan Paul, 1951), 101.
[50] Phillips, 'Religion and Epistemology: Some Contemporary Confusions', 127–8.
[51] Ibid. 128.     [52] Ibid. 129.

it have happened to me?' Phillips comments, 'I found this answer extremely impressive, *although I suspect that it needs a respect
for a certain kind of religious belief to find it so.*'[53] The other mother
had prayed to God for a son, and, when he was born, because he
was mentally handicapped, she rethought her attitude to prayer.
Rather than saying that God had sent her a mentally handicapped
son, she said that she had come closer to God and now knew what
it meant to cast a burden upon him. Phillips adds no such caveat
as he did with the previous mother, implying that he considers
this case to be a clear-cut example of religious belief.

This seems to me to sum up the bifurcation in Phillips extremely well. The third mother provides a definitive example of
religious belief; the second is religious for Phillips, but he can see
that other people might not find it so. On the one hand, we find
the definite distinction between true religion and superstition; on
the other, we find a personally interpreted distinction.

This personal distinction is religious rather than philosophical.
Philosophers are not in the business of making personal judgements. 'The philosopher is interested in looking at all these different perspectives, and removing knots: not judging them.'[54]

Since the philosopher cannot go further than grammatical
clarification, the debate between two grammatically unconfused
believers in God is a *religious* debate:

The difference between religious and non-religious perspectives is not
a philosophical difference. What separates them in their beliefs and
convictions is constitutive of their different ways of life. These different
ways of living are not interpretations of anything more ultimate than
themselves.[55]

The last sentence entails that there is no external perspective
from which an unconfused religious life-style can be judged. A
religious form of life is ultimately only responsible to its own
criteria, since there are no neutral or objective criteria which can
be applied to judge any life-style.

Thus, for Phillips, philosophy can show up some differences
between true religion and superstition, but the deeper meaning
of true religion is to be found in a religious context. Although
it is important not to foist one's own religious beliefs, such as

---

[53] Ibid. 128. My italics.    [54] Phillips, *Belief, Change and Forms of Life*, 118.
[55] Phillips, *Faith after Foundationalism*, 107.

observance of the sabbath, upon other religions which one does not fully understand, such as Buddhism, one can defend one's religious beliefs as true if challenged by an alternative religious viewpoint. Phillips writes:

What do I mean by 'true religion'? It seems to me that the question of truth cannot be answered in isolation from the content of religious beliefs and philosophical accounts of them. For example, if someone tells me that the barbaric practices of the early Hebrews reflect true religion more than the Passion of Christ, I can only ask him to look again. This does not mean that I have some independent criteria of judgment, some so-called rational standard. What it does mean is that I know something of the Passion of Christ, and that what I know makes me want to call this divine. A request for a further justification is simply misunderstanding masquerading as rationality.[56]

True religion, in this religious context, is a personal confession of what one knows (or, to the outsider, thinks one knows). There is no further justification than this personal knowledge from one's form of life. Seeking further justification is failing to know where to stop.

The fact that the issue of true religion depends upon one's personal response makes the fact of relativity appear to be a problem for Phillips's more positive claims. If there is no objective independent rational standard, then surely one's reactions to the appropriateness of the Proofs, for example, are as good as any other person's, as long as each reaction is grammatically unconfused. Yet we have seen that Phillips admits that conceptual analysis is subject to one's own personality, and is not a neutral activity, which keeps the fact of relativity to the fore.

In a sense, Phillips does accept the thinking of the cognitivists. They are right in their discussions if they are talking about a natural God, and a natural God only:

If a philosopher is aware that the God of whom he is giving an account is a natural God, an existent among existents, and an agent among agents, there is no philosophical objection to what he is doing. On the other hand, if he thinks that this conception of God is the only possible one, the only intelligible notion of divinity, he is making a mistake. Furthermore, if the philosopher proceeds to give an account of *all* conceptions of God in terms of a natural God, he is guilty of the naturalistic fallacy.[57]

---

[56] Phillips, *Religion and Understanding*, 6.      [57] Phillips, *The Concept of Prayer*, 158.

Kenny, for example, is guilty of this last fallacy with his refusal to accept that belief in God (that is, any God) can be acceptable without being rationally justified. This is simply to assume that if the conception of God with which one is familiar is unacceptable, then all conceptions of God are unacceptable: clearly a logical fallacy. However, Phillips himself is by no means free from the charge of giving a single account of all *genuine* conceptions of God. Clearly, the cognitivists do not think that they are discussing a natural God; and nothing in Phillips's conceptual analysis, depending as it does upon his own religious insights, is liable to convince them otherwise. For Phillips, the cognitivists simply fail to see something vital, something below the level of philosophical and even religious arguments:

What surprises me is that so many Christian philosophers seem to be talking about a natural, as opposed to supernatural, God; a God who is an existent among existents, and an agent among agents. What can one say to philosophers who insist on talking in this way? One can ask them to look again at the way people worship, and at what the Saints have written about their Faith. Also, one can point out the implications which their way of talking has for religion, and try to show how the implications of one's own views are truer to religious belief. On the other hand, one must not be afraid to admit that one's arguments about religion may reach a stage where all one can say to one's opponent is, 'Well, if you can't see it, that's that!'[58]

The point is that, of course, Phillips's critics are in the same position, and can equally well accuse Phillips of a lack of correct vision. If one's religious sympathies lie with Phillips's account of religion, then one will accept his position; while a sympathizer with his critics would accept his critics' position. Phillips's point is that ultimately this is a religious difference; in other words, it depends upon the form of life which gives rise to religion, and these forms of life will be different for different people. When we reach forms of life and the world pictures which rest upon them, we have reached bedrock; there can be no more discussion because the disagreement is too fundamental. It is a tautological truth that there can be nothing beneath bedrock.

The difficulty now is to see how one might proceed beyond relativity. Phillips admits that norms are simply what one

believes in; if one believes in a cognitive way, then one's normative conception of religion will be different from Phillips's. Yet
Phillips, while denying that bedrock presuppositions can be tested
(since no criteria of justification can be more fundamental than
bedrock), also denies that he, or Wittgenstein before him, is
stopping at relativity:

> In stressing the naturalness of our world-picture Wittgenstein is not
> establishing it as the *right* one. But in saying this Wittgenstein is not
> embracing a form of relativity. He is not saying that every person has
> a right or that every group has a right to his or their world-picture as
> the right one. . . . In noting changes in ways of thinking which may occur
> or have occurred, Wittgenstein is not testing hypotheses about the
> structure of the world. Rather, he is bringing out what is involved in
> these ways of thinking. He is not testing their foundations for they have
> no foundations.[59]

For Phillips, it seems, asserting the fact of relativity at a fundamental level is going too far. Different forms of life are simply
different forms of life; seeing them as having claims to validity
is to assume a bird's-eye view which does not exist. We, as language users, must stop with the form of life of which we are a
part. The fact of relativity does not run so deep because right and
wrong only make sense within a language game, not as part of
a foundation, for there are no foundations.

However, at another level—that of philosophical criticism—
the fact of relativity does appear to be relevant to Phillips's position. Is he asserting that his view of the appropriateness of the
Proofs is correct? If it is, then it seems as if Phillips must assume
that there is some standard to which he is adhering which makes
his account the (or a) correct one; for if he does not, then how can
he argue against the cognitivist tradition? Grammatical analysis
is, by his own admission, dependent upon one's personal insights;
and what makes Phillips's insights correct and the cognitivists'
incorrect? Certainly by Phillips's standards the cognitivist tradition
is in error; but is Phillips saying more than this in rejecting their
tradition?

I do not think that these questions are dealt with satisfactorily
by Phillips; much as the traditional philosophers of religion have
not dealt satisfactorily with Phillips's own position (as I have

---

[59] Phillips, *Faith after Foundationalism*, 63.

attempted to argue in this chapter). The reason for this, in my view, is the widespread philosophical rejection of the depth of relativity, and a failure to appreciate that relativity has many different forms and that different problems arise from and for each one. This oversight has been atoned for to an extent in recent years, and it is becoming clearer how varied relativity actually is. Without wishing to begin to take on board a discussion of these many varieties, I shall in the next chapter go on to look at a number of forms of relativity and will examine and reject a few attempted solutions to the problem of relativity. I shall try to show how the relativity which is germane to an acceptance of the appropriateness or inappropriateness of the Proofs within the Western philosophical tradition admits of no solution at all. I shall argue in future chapters that a proper acceptance of the problem of relativity brings us as close as we can to an assessment of the relevance of the Proofs of the existence of God.

# 4

# Relativity and Criteria

In the few works devoted to the subject, the fact of relativity and the doctrine of relativism are rarely kept apart. It is my intention in this chapter and the next to give a brief characterization of several types of relativism, and to adapt these to apply to the fact of relativity; to show the differences between relativism and relativity; and to construct an account of the implications of relativity by bringing out certain key notions of thinkers who have responded to it. Finally, in Chapter 6, I will apply the fruits of this discussion to Swinburne and Phillips, their philosophical schools, and the question of the appropriateness of the Proofs.

In discussing the fact of relativity, I employ the thinking of Wilhelm Dilthey to illustrate the relativity of criteria, particularly philosophical criteria; Gordon Kaufman to show the authority of criteria; Richard Rorty and Wittgenstein to distinguish between situations in which there are common criteria and situations in which there are not; and Joseph Runzo to distinguish between absolutes *per se* and personal absolutes. In the light of these discussions, I shall adumbrate my own conception of fundamental trust, showing its difference from basic belief and groundless belief; and argue for its relevance to the central debate between Swinburne and Phillips.

## 1. TYPES OF RELATIVISM

In this section, I shall give a typology of relativism, based largely upon the divisions of relativism to be found in the literature.[1] I

---

[1] Particularly Jack W. Meiland and Michael Krausz (eds.), *Relativism: Cognitive and Moral* (Notre Dame, Ind.: University of Notre Dame Press, 1982); Joseph Margolis, *Pragmatism without Foundations* (New York and Oxford: Basil Blackwell, 1986); Martin Hollis and Steven Lukes (eds.), *Rationality and Relativism* (Oxford: Basil Blackwell, 1982); Joseph Runzo, *Reason, Relativism and God* (Basingstoke: Macmillan, 1986).

shall ignore the many types of relativism which have no relevance to my argument, such as moral relativism and value relativism; hence my typology is not intended to be exhaustive. I shall also attempt to translate these types of relativism into types of relativity, giving arguments for why this needs to be done.

### (i) *Protagorean relativism*

First, I wish to deal briefly with the variety of relativism which has been widely and easily dismissed, and is often thought to be the only variety. I shall label this Protagoreanism, following Joseph Margolis, although whether this accurately represents the view of Protagoras is not my concern here. Protagoreanism is the theory that every belief, or assertion, or piece of knowledge, is as good as every other; in other words, is as true, or as right, or as appropriate. Philosophers have found it a straightforward task to demonstrate the self-referential incoherence of such a theory. To hold that all knowledge, truth, etc. is relative, in the sense that all claims to knowledge are equally good, begs the question of the nature of the claim that all knowledge is relative. The initial claim of Protagoreanism is absolute or non-relative (I use 'absolute' to mean simply 'non-relative' throughout these chapters), yet its own assertion is that all claims are relative. Hence the self-referential incoherence of Protagorean relativism.

The mistake which many philosophers have made is to assume that Protagoreanism is the only form of relativism, or that all other types of relativism are reducible to it. Richard Rorty ridicules Protagorean relativism for being a view which 'no one holds', adding that, 'except for the occasional cooperative freshman, one cannot find anybody who says that two incompatible opinions on an important topic are equally good'.[2] Rorty thinks that he dismisses relativism from being akin to his own theory of pragmatism by refuting Protagoreanism. Fortunately, the few more deeply searching articles and books on the subject belie this opinion, putting forward a great variety of theories of relativism quite distinct from Protagoreanism. Alasdair Macintyre, writing with characteristic and refreshing candour, expresses deep suspicion of thinking that one has refuted relativism by refuting the Protagorean version:

[2] Richard Rorty, *Consequences of Pragmatism: Essays 1972–1980* (Brighton: Harvester, 1982), 166.

*Relativity and Criteria*

Relativism, like scepticism, is one of those doctrines that have now been refuted a number of times too often. Nothing is perhaps a surer sign that a doctrine embodies some not-to-be-neglected truth than that in the course of the history of philosophy it should be refuted again and again. Genuinely refutable doctrines only need to be refuted once.[3]

It is the 'not-to-be-neglected truth' of relativism, to be found in non-Protagorean versions, to which I now turn.

### (ii) *Conceptual relativism*

I use this label to refer to a broad family of different but connected theories. The basic thesis is that perceptions, perspectives, truth, knowledge, rationality, and so on[4] are relative to individual and or social conceptual frameworks, paradigms, forms of life, mental experience, culture, world views, world pictures, language games, and so on.[5] Exactly which label is used to refer to the framework that truth is relative to is a matter of dispute, as is the nature of the framework: whether it is completely or primarily linguistic or practical or subjective, and so on. The nature of the frameworks is itself as subject to relativism as truth is.

A useful distinction can be made, however, between individual conceptual relativism and social conceptual relativism. The former states that truth is relative to an individual's conceptual framework. In other words, the nature of truth is relative to one's own cognitive make-up, one's own collection of concepts, one's own way of reasoning. One could label this cognitive relativism, being a thesis which reflects upon mental and intellectual states. The latter asserts that truth is relative to a social framework, one comprising upbringing, social consensus, past history of one's culture, current social trends, and so on. One can usefully label this cultural relativism, since it is a thesis about cultural influences upon individuals and society. Conceptual relativism is a

---

[3] Alasdair Macintyre, 'Relativism, Power and Philosophy', in *Proceedings and Addresses of The American Philosophical Association*, 1985, p. 5.

[4] To avoid inelegant repetition, I shall only refer to 'truth', but shall mean by it in this context all the components of this list.

[5] For this list, I shall use 'conceptual frameworks' as I use 'truth' above.

view which is most plausibly seen to combine cognitive and cultural relativism, i.e. to combine the relativity of truth to individual and social frameworks, and to the influence of the individual upon the social and vice versa.

### (iii) *Preconceptual relativism*

This form of relativism needs to be carefully distinguished from the previous form. It is closer to subjectivism than conceptual relativism is, and refers more to individuals than society. The theory is that truth is relative to one's dispositions, insights, intuitions, or character. Cognitive relativism is a theory about a person's intellectual make-up, while preconceptual relativism deals with the pre-intellectual, or perhaps emotional aspects of a person. It need not be seen as being in competition with any form of conceptual relativism: the overall thesis of relativism could be that truth is relative to one's intellectual and emotional frameworks.

### (iv) *Epistemological relativism*

I use this label to refer to a number of different but connected theories. The essential component which links them all is the claim that the criteria used for making judgements, for asserting what knowledge is and what one knows, for asserting the nature of truth and what is true, are relative to conceptual frameworks. Again, the nature of the framework that criteria are relative to is itself subject to the fact of relativity.

One can subdivide epistemological relativism in a similar manner to conceptual relativism. Individual epistemological relativism, which I label internal relativism (thus departing from Margolis's use of the term), is the thesis that criteria for truth are relative to one's own conceptual framework. Social epistemological relativism, which I label external relativism (again departing from Margolis), is the thesis that criteria for truth are relative to social frameworks. Again, there is no requirement to make this distinction completely exclusive; one can combine external and internal relativism to comprise epistemological relativism, which allows for the interaction between individuals and society.

## (v) *Surface and depth relativism*

A further distinction can be made which applies to the three kinds of relativism already listed. This is between what I shall call surface and depth relativism. The former refers to the relativity of different claims which are held to be true: if I hold $x$ to be true, and you hold $y$ to be true, and there appears to be no possibility of agreement. The latter refers to the relativity of claims to what counts as truth itself: if I hold that truth is pragmatic viability and you hold that it is correspondence to external reality, and there appears to be no possibility of agreement. Surface relativism assumes some sort of consensus upon what constitutes truth; depth relativism questions that very consensus.

## (vi) *Incommensurability and relativity*

Armed with this battery of distinctions, I shall now distinguish between relativism and relativity. I am not aware of a clear distinction being made between these two in the literature; nor do I suppose that all writers who have written upon relativism have discussed relativism as I define it. (Indeed, many, in discussing relativism, have been concerned with what I call relativity.)

The essential difference between relativism and relativity as I draw it is that only the former holds to the incommensurability thesis. This is the thesis, for my purposes, that different conceptual frameworks *cannot* be translated one into another. The relativity of conceptual frameworks becomes the last word if we view relativism as true, because this is the inescapable consequence of the incommensurability thesis.

Relativism understood thus has a non-relative bias built into it. Incommensurability becomes the situation beyond which it is impossible to go. Debates between people or societies of different conceptual frameworks will always and unavoidably founder. Thus relativism is not a purely descriptive thesis about the diversity of conceptual frameworks, insights, and sets of criteria, but is also a positive thesis about diversity being the ineluctable final word.

I contrast this with relativity, which is a description and not a positive thesis. The fact of relativity entails an acceptance of the divergences between cultures and individuals, and concentrates upon particular instances (such as the Swinburne and Phillips debate) to see if in some way they have solved, dissolved, or transcended the fact of relativity. The fact of relativity is itself treated as relative. Relativity may not be the last word: perhaps God, a Platonic Idea, absolute Reason, or an awareness of some non-relative error within relativity, may illustrate how relativity is to be overcome. As I have drawn the distinction, relativism does not treat itself as relative: rather, it claims that all claims are relative, except its own. Relativism is not relative. The fact of relativity, which does take itself as (possibly) relative, thus casts doubt upon the positive thesis of relativism. It refers to a possibly revisable description, not a definitive theory.

One can reformulate the typology of relativism which I have given as a typology of relativity. Instead of the typology referring to theses which hold to the inescapability of the divergence of conceptual frameworks, one can reformulate the typology to refer to descriptions of ways in which frameworks do diverge, without holding to any thesis about the finality of such divergences.

Thus, conceptual relativism can be reformulated as conceptual relativity, the *thesis* of truth as relative to conceptual frameworks being replaced by a relative *description* of truth as relative to conceptual frameworks. The difference is that within conceptual relativism, relativity is a situation which cannot be transcended or dissolved; whereas within conceptual relativity, relativity could perhaps be transcended or dissolved, because relativity is not seen as a non-relative fact. This reformulation can be performed for any of the four forms of relativism, and their subdivisions, which I have discussed.

I now wish to examine the work of several thinkers who have felt the need to respond to relativity in some way. Many of them write about 'relativism', and I shall keep their word when quoting from their writings, but my discussion, for reasons given in this section, is actually concerned with the fact of relativity. Although I argue that all the thinkers whom I discuss have failed to provide a fully adequate response to the fact of relativity, I argue further that each thinker illustrates some important feature for a properly adequate response. I will attempt to bring out these features in this and the next chapter before applying them to the appropriateness of the Proofs in the final chapter.

## 2. THE RELATIVITY OF PHILOSOPHICAL CRITERIA

The majority of philosophers, including Swinburne and Phillips and the schools of which they are a part, have felt that the use of certain criteria overcomes the fact of relativity. In other words, they dispute the fact of epistemological relativity. When a philosophical dispute occurs, it is widely held that the best manner of resolution is by appealing to criteria common to all philosophy.

Some philosophers have attempted to provide a list of such criteria. R. C. Marsh, for example, refers to logical validity, consistency, and correspondence to the evidence of the senses.[6] Nicholas Rescher gives a far longer list, including 'formal criteria like consistency, uniformity (treating like cases alike), comprehensiveness, systematic elegance, simplicity, economy (Ockham's razor, etc.)' and 'material criteria like closeness to common sense, explanatory adequacy, inherent plausibility, allocations of presumption, and burden of proof, etc.'.[7] Rescher adds that there is a certain 'relativity in the value standards of philosophical argumentation'[8] because not all philosophers agree over the balance of these measures.

Such a caveat is rarely given in philosophical discussions of relativity. The widespread assumption is that some list of criteria, such as Marsh or Rescher provides, is valid beyond the strictures of the fact of relativity as I have outlined it. This is an assumption infrequently argued for, partly, as I have suggested, because of a failure within philosophy to distinguish between relativism and relativity. I wish to examine the relevance of the fact of relativity to philosophical criteria in this section, by outlining a highly instructive failure to respond to this fact in the work of Wilhelm Dilthey, and applying my criticisms of Dilthey to the philosophies of Swinburne and Phillips in particular.

### (i) Erlebnis *and* Weltanschauungslehre

Dilthey is a particularly important figure in the history of relativity, for he was the first thinker of the modern era to combine

---

[6] R. C. Marsh, 'The Function of Criticism in Philosophy', *Proceedings of the Aristotelian Society*, 53 (1953), 140–2.

[7] Nicholas Rescher, 'Philosophical Disagreement', *Renew of Metaphysics*, 32 (1978), 225.                                              [8] Ibid. 228 n.

a depth of knowledge in a diversity of areas with an awareness of the philosophical importance of such diversity. His very interest in a considerable number of diverse areas of knowledge made him aware of the seeming impossibility of constructing a single truth or employing a criterion of truth beyond the relativity of a particular time, place, and personality.

Dilthey groups the major types of diverse attitudes to the world into three *Weltanschauungen,* or world views. Briefly, these are naturalism (a primarily cognitive outlook reducing mental and spiritual elements, moral and aesthetic values to physical reality), subjective idealism (a primarily emotive world view placing mind and spirit above physical reality), and objective idealism (primarily conative, a contemplative and aesthetic perspective uniting the mental and the physical into one reality).

The merit of the theory of world views is that it clearly reveals competing claims to absolute truth. Each of the three types of world view sees itself as possessing the absolute truth, and we as human beings are not in a neutral position from which to be able to judge between them. The relativity of all claims to the absolute now seems firmly established. The worry here, which is the worry for any genuine acceptance of the fact of relativity, is how it can be possible to avoid the chaos of decision making which the fact of relativity seems to entail. As Dilthey writes, given the relativity of world views, 'where are the means to overcome the anarchy of opinions which then threaten to befall us?'.[9]

His answer is that, by means of a studying of the world views, or *Weltanschauungslehre,* it is possible to discern a non-relative element undergirding them all. This element is *Erlebnis,* or lived experience; in other words, it is the direct perception of life rather than life itself. It is the interface of inner life and external reality, and as such is a universal human phenomenon.

*Erlebnis* becomes the criterion upon which all relative human world views can be judged. Study of humanity and the expression vouchsafed by great art give us our closest glimpse of the content of *Erlebnis.* All knowledge contained within the *Weltanschauungen* is relative, and yet the 'anarchy of opinions' is

[9] Quoted in Rudolf Makkreel, *Dilthey: Philosopher of the Human Studies,* (Princeton, NJ: Princeton University Press, 1975), 3.

prevented by the only unconditional human phenomenon, lived experience.

This brief sketch cannot do justice to the breadth and profundity of Dilthey's work, but it is sufficient to illustrate how difficult it is to overcome the fact of relativity. Dilthey's choice of a criterion to perform this task is itself open to criticisms, which are in turn instructive for an assessment of any attempt to provide non-relative criteria in opposition to relativity.

### (ii) *Dilthey is limited to his society's world view*

There is a tension in Dilthey's thought, as in any serious account of relativity, between the need to defend relativity and the need, which Dilthey identified, to assert something absolute. Dilthey constantly expressed a confidence in the power of the human sciences which was never more than a reflection of the general optimism of his era in studies of man. Freud, Durkheim, and naturalistic thinkers generally reflect a move away from theocentricity towards anthropocentricity. Dilthey is a part of such a move, but he does not always seem to recognize the culturally relative nature of his confidence in the unconditionality of the results of the *Geisteswissenschaften*, or human studies. Indeed, during his lifetime, he altered his idea of what would count as the science which accurately described *Erlebnis*, and thus undergirded the other sciences, from psychology via phenomenalism to hermeneutics. This illustrates the general problem of searching for an unconditional foundational method of investigation which accurately represents the absolute or the universal. The confidence in science fulfilling this role has been cogently questioned by thinkers such as Popper, Kuhn, and Polanyi, who have emphasized the inescapability of the humanity of the scientist. Human beings are culturally limited, and it needs a far more subtle account of an activity transcending such limits than Dilthey provides for science to overcome the problem of relativity. The standards of one society will not necessarily be the standards of another. The fact of cultural relativity has been underemphasized in Dilthey's thought.

Dilthey provides a more promising suggestion with his account of art. We think of great writers having more to say than they consciously intended when writing: this is a hallmark of greatness. Dilthey emphasizes the non-relativity of artistic insight, yet this does not overcome the fact of relativity because insight itself is subject to preconceptual relativity. The aesthetic may overcome any form of conceptual relativity, with its emphasis upon the cognitive and cultural, but it does not overcome any relativity which is concerned with the preconceptual level.

Similarly, Swinburne reflects a widespread modern confidence in the efficacy of logic and mathematics to resolve issues of seeming impenetrability. Dilthey's confidence in the *Geisteswissenschaften* is mirrored in Swinburne's trust in the power of logical argument and the reasoning ability of the human mind.

Phillips, alternatively, decries such confidence, and is more akin to Dilthey's attitude to art with his positive response to, and widespread use of, literature to support his philosophical points. In this he mirrors the philosophical movements such as existentialism, in which Camus and Sartre, most famously, wrote novels and plays to encapsulate their philosophical points. Mann, Dostoevsky, and Tolstoy, for example, exemplify a great European tradition of philosophizing in literature. The relativistic worry with these thinkers is that the aesthetic is open to preconceptual relativity to the same extent that the rationalistic arguments of a philosopher like Swinburne are open to cultural relativity.

### (iii) *Dilthey is limited to his own personal view*

There is another tension in Dilthey between the relativity of world views and the possibility of going beyond them. He disputes the metaphysical attempt to find an absolute view of the world, and yet deems it possible to see the relativity of world views by means of the *Weltanschauungslehre*. This is a tension for any theory of relativism, rather than for the fact of relativity. On the one hand it must be held that our beliefs, perspectives, and so on are relative to our conceptual frameworks, but, on the other, the relativist must have a perspective on the presence of the world views which is not relative. In attempting to resolve relativism, Dilthey has simply reaffirmed relativity.

Although Dilthey did not strictly align himself with any of the world views, it is clear from his writings that he is primarily an objective idealist. Commenting upon a dream that had a

particular influence upon Dilthey, one of his critics, Theodore
Plantinga, makes clear this preference:

It was not his task as a philosopher to advocate a particular world view,
but in his non-philosophical writings especially, his preference became
clear.... He had personally chosen for the world view of the thinkers
who attracted him most (i.e. Schleiermacher, Goethe and Hegel). In other
words, his own outlook represents what he called objective idealism.[10]

Swinburne and Phillips, although their world views may not
fit snugly into Dilthey's typology of *Weltanschauungen*, do not
sufficiently admit to the relevance of their own personal outlooks to their philosophical writings. Swinburne has much sympathy with the medieval period in which God was perceived to
be within the purview of logical arguments and detailed analysis
of the minutiae of religious language was encouraged. Equally,
Swinburne is personally disinclined to the post-Enlightenment
scepticism against such medieval confidence. These personal
preferences clearly contribute to relativizing Swinburne's preferred conceptions of God and of proper philosophy.

Phillips's sympathies lie with the indirect method of philosophy and a conception of the mysterious nature of God. He has
no leaning towards Swinburne's confidence in the great extent of
the power of philosophy to resolve contentious issues of existence, such as the existence of God. Nor does he sympathize with
the medieval and rationalistic concern to give a detailed exposition
of a clearly defined concept of God. In these personal world views,
Phillips and Swinburne demonstrate an inability to go beyond
the apparent relativism of the *Weltanschauungen*, by being unable
to interact sufficiently with each other's outlooks. This is a point
which I shall return to in the next two chapters.

### (iv) *Dilthey's choice of* Erlebnis *is relative*

The key concept in Dilthey's overcoming of relativism is that
of *Erlebnis*. This is supposed to provide the universal link which
binds mankind, and direct apprehension of it provides an awareness which is not relative. The problem lies with the worry that

---

[10] Theodore Plantinga, *Historical Understanding in the Thought of Wilhelm Dilthey*
(Toronto: University of Toronto Press, 1980), 144–5.

the check upon relativism is actually a result of Dilthey's own, relative world view of objective idealism.

It is not surprising that Dilthey saw man's common link as something in experience. Equally it should not be surprising that those people whose sympathies lie with naturalism or subjective idealism would find some quite different common link for mankind: our purely physical interactions or our purely spiritual life respectively. To adopt any of these attributes as common links of mankind is to adopt a certain *Weltanschauung*: and this is precisely what Dilthey himself has done. Thus it becomes difficult to see how Dilthey's arguments about *Erlebnis* genuinely break free from the fact of relativity.

The same problem bedevils Swinburne and Phillips. Swinburne adopts accounts of religious language as the criterion upon which to construct a conception of God, while Phillips prefers the criterion of primary religious language. Each criterion can be seen to be relative to its respective social and personal world view, Swinburne with his insistence upon refined, clarified, and exact religious language and Phillips with his preference for original, uninterpreted religious language spoken in its worshipful context.

### (v) *Dilthey's philosophy of religion is relative*

In a similar vein to his confidence in the *Geisteswissenschaften*, Dilthey also trusted in a particular philosophical heritage and a particular set of philosophical problems as being handed down for all time. Dilthey assimilates the critical, epistemological concerns of Kant, the French positivist confidence in science, and the British empiricist concern with the study of the contents of the mind. He is overwhelmed by the philosophical concern with man and his experience: 'man is the one true beginning of knowledge'.[11] He relies unquestioningly upon the immanence of subjects for study; he does not see the relativity of such philosophical concern.

This is a problem for philosophy generally. The empiricist tradition, of which Swinburne is a part, tends to see philosophical

---

[11] Quoted in Michael Ermath, *Wilhelm Dilthey: The Critique of Historical Reason* (Chicago: University of Chicago Press, 1978), 21. Translated by the author, from *Gesammelte Schriften*, xviii, 208.

problems as independent of their historical context. To assess the validity of an argument and investigate its historical context are two different activities for this kind of philosophy, the former being the more important. This view faces the objection that the problems of philosophy are not universal and unconditional: that the nature of arguments, and the methods of assessing arguments, are relative to culture, conceptual frameworks, differing paradigms of rationality, and so on.

Meanwhile, the Wittgensteinian school faces an opposite problem. It accepts the contingency of language and the impossibility of philosophy going further than describing, and sometimes assessing, language use. It portrays the immanentist bias of Dilthey: that philosophy cannot go beyond man's language to make any useful study. The problem here is to see why language should be seen as the stopping point. Dilthey chose *Erlebnis* seemingly because of his relative world view; and it appears as if the Wittgensteinians have an equally relative world view which cannot allow any remotely traditional transcendence of language. To these problems I shall return in Chapter 6.

### (vi) *Dilthey's rejection of religion is relative*

Dilthey often wrote as if the *Weltanschauungslehre* heralded the end for religious belief. 'If historical and psychological relativism were the last word, it would touch the religions first of all.'[12] This is because Dilthey sees religion as entailing an absolute belief in God, whereas the only absolute is that which undergirds all *Weltanschauungen*, namely *Erlebnis*. Dilthey gives a historical critique of religions to show that religious experience is a cultural, institutionalized phenomenon. From a historical investigation, it can be seen that the transcendent is a projection from our own experience. Religion needs to posit a beyond to safeguard hope in the face of earthly suffering.

Such a rejection of the transcendence vouchsafed by religion is a consequence of Dilthey's refusal to look beyond man's *Erlebnis* as the ultimate subject for study. 'Every effort of comprehension

---

[12] Quoted in H. A. Hodges, *The Philosophy of Wilhelm Dilthey* (London: Routledge and Kegan Paul, 1952), 314. Translated by the author, from *GS* vii, page number not given by the translator.

goes out from the world of the here and now; man who constantly lives in the world and is constantly moved to inquiry by it does not live in the transcendent.'[13] Dilthey holds dogmatically to the principle that there is nothing for man beyond experience. Although this can be agreed upon by objective idealists and naturalists, the subjective idealist need not accept any such principle. The difficulty is to see how Dilthey's own principle can avoid the trap of relativity and the slide into dogmatism. It seems that it is caught in this situation: all Dilthey's references to a viewpoint beyond the *Weltanschauungen*—in other words, a viewpoint which could see the relativity of the world views—come to nothing because his own remarks are clearly within rather than without the *Weltanschauungen*. This casts severe doubts upon the non-relativity of Dilthey's rejection of religion.

It seems that Dilthey himself experienced such doubts. He is aware that the decline of religious experience is in part a product of his own epoch:

The possibility of experiencing religious states in my own existence is for me, as for most men today, strictly limited. But when I run through the letters and writings of Luther, the reports of his contemporaries, the records of the religious conferences and councils and of his official activities I experience a religious process of such eruptive power, of such energy, in which life and death are at stake, that it lies beyond all possibility of being actually lived through by a man of our day. But I can re-live it. . . . And so this process opens up to us a religious world in him and in his contemporaries of early Reformation times, which broadens our horizon to include the possibilities of human life which only so become accessible to us.[14]

In a sense, then, Dilthey's rejection of religion is no more than a relative reflection of his own social situation, and a consequence of him limiting himself to a purely historical assessment of religion. There are indications that he, as a person, would have liked to have been able to be religious:

Is not my own historical standpoint a fruitless scepticism, if I measure it against such a life [referring to a Christian friend]? We must endure

[13] Dilthey, *Der Junge Dilthey: Letters and Diary 1852–1870*, selected by Clara Misch-Dilthey (Leipzig and Berlin, 1933), 152.
[14] Quoted in Hodges, *The Philosophy of Wilhelm Dilthey*, 276–7. Translated by the author, from *GS* vii, 215–16.

and conquer this world, we must act upon it. How victoriously my friend does so. Where in my *Weltanschauung* is there a like power?[15]

He cannot accept religion, because he cannot accept that its claims are anything more than relative. Yet if my argument is correct, Dilthey's claims are no more than relative themselves.

Dilthey admitted that there were things about Christianity that he could not understand. This is partly because of Dilthey's over-emphasis upon the aesthetic. He wrote that the music of Bach seemed to him more religious than the writings of Luther,[16] and the reason for this must partly be that, for him, art was far more capable of expressing universal validity than religion was. In this he continued the trend in German philosophy to value art more highly than religion, found in Schopenhauer and Nietzsche, for example. However, anyone more sympathetic to religion than art could reverse this standpoint and argue that religion is better able than art to express universal validity. Dilthey could either accept this point of view as equally valid, thus embracing relativity, or he could reject it, but only by a dogmatic retreat to the principle that there is nothing for man beyond *Erlebnis*. He cannot reject God as such an ultimate stopping point other than by an expression of his own relative *Weltanschauung*.

The problem is by no means limited to Dilthey. The worry is that the ultimate stopping point, beyond which enquiry makes no sense—be it reason, language, man, experience, or God—is a reflection of a relative world view. Rather than providing an absolute element which prevents the full import of the fact of relativity, it appears that all such stopping points are illustrations of that fact. Dilthey's conception of God is derived from a historical point of view, and by being limited to being no more than a historical conception, God is denied transcendence. Dilthey has a relative conception of God; but, following on from my previous discussion, this applies to Phillips and Swinburne also. There is no definitive empirical check upon the word 'God', as I have argued,[17] and the worries are that each conception of God is relative to a particular tradition, and that the criteria to be

[15] Quoted in Hodges, *The Philosophy of Wilhelm Dilthey*, 314. Translated by the author, from *GS* vii, page number not given by translator.

[16] See Makkreel, *Dilthey: Philosopher of the Human Studies*, 367.

[17] See Ch. 3, sect. 1(i).

used in assessing 'true' religion or an 'accurate' conception of God are similarly relative. The specific problems infecting Dilthey's thinking reflect general problems which bedevil the schools of philosophy concerned with the question of the appropriateness of the Proofs.


## 3. THE AUTHORITY OF CRITERIA

The relativity of criteria, and philosophical criteria in particular, leaves open the question of how we should treat the status of criteria, and consequently the status of our judgements. I contend that Gordon Kaufman provides a useful suggestion here concerning the authority which we should bestow upon our criteria for making judgements, and it is to a consideration of his writings that I now turn.[18]

Kaufman's useful suggestion, however, does not remove him from the problematic relativistic situation which we are discussing. He shares many objections to the appropriateness of the Proofs with the Wittgensteinian school: God is a presupposition and not an inference;[19] God is unknowable and inexpressible;[20] God is not an existent;[21] and truth is not correspondence to an external paradigm of reality.[22] The problem of these objections being relative to a particular, disputable conception of God and language has already been mentioned.[23]

Similarly, much of Kaufman's positive writing about God falters for reasons similar to Dilthey's: for example, he trusts the results of immanent, historical critiques to provide a definite conception of God;[24] and he too gives a characterization of world views (the secular, seeing only this world, the theistic, seeing another world, and the religious, which scorns the two-world distinction) yet implicitly asserts a particular relative world view

---

[18] Especially *God: The Problem* (Cambridge, Mass.: Harvard University Press, 1972), *The Theological Imagination* (Philadelphia: The Westminster Press, 1981), and *Systematic Theology* (New York: Charles Scribner's Sons, 1968).

[19] Kaufman, 'The Foundations of Belief', in *God: The Problem*, 254.

[20] Kaufman accepts the distinction between the noumenal and the phenomenal God.          [21] Kaufman, *The Theological Imagination*, 82.

[22] Again, Kaufman is a Kantian here.          [23] See Ch. 3, Sect. 4.

[24] Kaufman, 'Transcendence without Mythology', in *God: The Problem*, 46.

above the others by holding, at least in the epistemological realm, to the priority of the secular.[25]

Despite these faults, however, Kaufman provides an important but difficult consideration concerning relativity. His writing is much concerned with possibly the most important type of relativity for our discussion of the Proofs, namely epistemological relativity. It is concerned less with truth than with the criteria we employ for judging what is true. Kaufman's argument is that these criteria have authority for us. 'Everyone stands under some authority in the sense of more or less spontaneously turning in some *particular direction* to some *particular locus* when he seeks truth: to sense experience or scientific method, to logical or semantic analysis, to psychoanalysis or aesthetic insight.'[26] One could add to this list analytical reason (in the case of Swinburne) and grammatical analysis (in the case of Phillips).

The point is that the choice of these criteria is a relative one. No one authority has more non-relative adequacy than others: our choice of criteria is simply relative to our culture, background, and experience.[27] The authority of the criteria we use rests beyond rational proof; rather, it is revealed to us. This revelation cannot be justified because our criteria for making judgements depend upon such revelation. 'By "revelation" we are intending to designate the source and ground of the very criteria to which one might appeal in such proof.'[28]

Although Kaufman chooses theological language to make his epistemological points (he also refers to the mystery of why we choose one set of criteria rather than another as 'the mystery of election'[29]), this is not necessary. One can rephrase Kaufman's point as being that the criteria we use to make judgements, even to give content to apparently fundamental concepts such as truth and proof, lie beyond any such concepts. Thus, they are subject to epistemological relativity, because any appeal to one set of criteria rather than another can only be relative to one's conceptual framework, since we have no way of going beyond all our criteria in order to give a non-relative judgement about them.

In my view, Kaufman has briefly and inchoately sketched an

[25] This assertion occurs in connection with his choice of rationality as the basic criterion over and above feeling, willing, and so on: 'The only normative grounding actually available to humans [is] rational critical analysis and reflection' (*The Theological Imagination*, 253).          [26] Kaufman, *Systematic Theology*, 65.
[27] Ibid.      [28] Ibid. 22.      [29] Ibid. 65.

account of relativity and a response to it more cogent than his prolific writings on pragmatic tests and the noumenal God intended to keep relativity in check. An account of the way in which the authority of criteria is revealed can only be relative. 'The interpretation of revelation to which we come can never be more or other than the understanding which *we* have in *our* situation in history with *our* experience of the world as mediated to us through *our* aptitudes and biases and intellect.'[30] Thus, Kaufman implicitly accepts all the kinds of relativity listed earlier in this chapter.

The fact of the fundamental authority of criteria has to be trusted in as non-relative. Criteria will change, but there must be some criterion or set of criteria taken to be non-relative or else no one could hold any beliefs at all. The analogy of Neurath's ship is appropriate here: one cannot examine all the planks of the ship at the same time, because one must rest unquestioningly on some planks in order to examine any others. It is my contention that neither Swinburne nor Phillips, nor the schools in which they stand, have taken this point seriously enough.

Kaufman hints at my own notion of fundamental trust, to be discussed in the next chapter, when he argues that, because of relativity, it is an act of faith or trust to suppose that that which one takes to be true, or to constitute truth, really is true or is an adequate conception of truth. This applies to concepts such as knowledge, rationality, and justification also. The fact of relativity prevents us from taking criteria on anything more than trust. Were relativism true, then the non-relative truth of relativism itself could be taken as a piece of definite knowledge. However, in the case of relativity, the fact of relativity can be held in no more than a relative way. Definite, non-relative knowledge is apparently denied; therefore one can only have trust in relation to the relativity of relativity. This trust must take something as non-relative; if it takes $x$ as non-relative it can do no more than trust that $x$ is non-relative. I shall go on to discuss this more fully in Chapter 5.

In this chapter, I have argued that the simple listing of philosophical criteria intended to overcome the fact of relativity will not do. For not only do philosophers disagree over the balance of criteria, but even over which criteria are relevant and

---

[30] Ibid. 74.

what constitutes a particular criterion. Thus some philosophers (sceptics) would deny that closeness to common sense is an adequate criterion; some (Phillips, for instance) would deny systematic elegance; while others (Swinburne and Mackie over Occam's razor, for example) would disagree over what a particular criterion constitutes.[31] This divergence is below the level of deciding upon criteria; it is at the level at which there is trust in something upon which the rest of the philosopher's thinking can develop. Thus, attempting to list criteria to help resolve philosophical divergence is not useful in such situations of disparity.

This is even true of an apparently straightforward and incontrovertible criterion such as the need for cogent arguments. Not only do philosophers disagree over the interpretation of what an argument is—one could compare Swinburne's probabilistic calculus with Kierkegaard's indirect communication—but also over the importance of argument at all. Phillips, for instance, sometimes relies solely upon examples to make a point, while Sartre often prefers to present a situation rather than construct an argument. Rorty writes amusingly that analytical philosophers cannot find 'anything they would consider an *argument* in a carload of Heidegger or Foucault'.[32]

The tendency of much philosophy is to move from taking its criteria as authoritative (as Kaufman shows cannot be avoided) to taking its criteria as the only appropriate ones. The influence of one's personality, background, social culture, religious and philosophical beliefs, and so on, casts doubt upon the possibility of providing a non-relative set of criteria for making philosophical judgements. Nietzsche saw the unavoidably personal and social composition of philosophy: 'Gradually it has become clear to me what every great philosophy so far has been: namely, the personal confession of its author and a kind of involuntary and unconscious memoir.'[33] The quotation applies as much to Nietzsche, of course, as to every other philosopher.

---

[31] As noted previously, Mackie takes Occam's razor in the traditional formulation of not allowing into one's explanation anything more than is strictly necessary. Swinburne reinterprets Occam's razor as the principle of simplicity, which commends the simplest possible final explanation of any phenomenon.

[32] Rorty, *Consequences of Pragmatism*, 224.

[33] Friedrich Nietzsche, *Beyond Good and Evil*, trans. Helen Zimmern (Edinburgh and London: T. N. Foulis, 1909), 13.

The importance of the relativity of philosophical criteria for our present discussion is twofold. First, it shows that, in purely philosophical debates, there will be divergence over judging what philosophy should be doing and by what methods. Such divergence is a consequence of the fact of epistemological relativity, of both internal and external forms. Philosophical criteria are not unconditionally given for every philosopher of every era for every context; rather, they are relative to individual character and background, the relevant historical period, current social influences, and philosophical schools.

Secondly, it illustrates how a philosophical solution to a problem such as the appropriateness of the Proofs can only be relative. Swinburne gives no suggestion that his philosophical discussion is relative to his own personal and cultural situation; and Phillips's suggestions about this, as I shall argue in Chapter 6, are explicitly rejected by his own denial of relativity. However, Swinburne and Phillips are making philosophical judgements about the appropriateness of the Proofs: and these judgements are based upon their own relative philosophical criteria.

This suggests that there simply is no answer to the general question 'are the Proofs of God's existence theologically and philosophically appropriate?'. In each instance, we need to relate the question to a personal, cultural, or historical situation, to a particular religious or philosophical framework, to whether the question is intended as metaphysical, historical, or religious. For instance, the question of whether the Proofs are appropriate to a Cartesian, Enlightenment project is different from the question of whether the Proofs are appropriate to post-modern philosophy. The question is different for a Methodist from what it is for a Quaker, for someone taught at Oxford from someone taught in South America, for a person in a liberal culture from someone in an oppressive one. What is important is not simply to perform historical, philosophical, and religious investigation so that we can answer these questions, but also to assess whether the Proofs are appropriate (or should be appropriate) to us as individuals or communities in our current personal and cultural situations, with all the ideas of the nature of God, the meaning of religious language, and the role of philosophy which these entail.

# 5

# Trust and Disagreement

In the previous chapter I argued that the consequences of several forms of relativity are to reveal the relativity of philosophical criteria and the consequent relativity of solutions to the question of the appropriateness of the Proofs. I have done this primarily by concentrating upon the lessons to be learned from both the cogent arguments and the errors of Dilthey and Kaufman. I also made a point to be brought out more fully in this chapter, that because of the fact of relativity we have to trust in the authority of the criteria, philosophical and otherwise, which we use for making judgements. In this chapter I shall also consider the merits and demerits of Richard Rorty and Joseph Runzo in responding to relativity, bringing out their respective useful distinctions between normal and abnormal discourse, and universal and personal absolutes, before using the positive elements of the discussion to expound my own conception of fundamental trust.

## 1. DIVERGENT DISCOURSE

In this section I shall give a brief account of what I take to be the errors in Rorty's response to relativity, before giving an exposition of his useful distinction between normal and abnormal discourse. I shall then relate this distinction to my own between disagreement and disparity, showing how it is similar to and yet different from Wittgenstein's understanding of disagreement.

### (i) *Normal and abnormal discourse*

Although, as already mentioned,[1] Rorty gives a brief and unsatisfactory rejection of relativity, reducing it to Protagorean relativism, his positive account of pragmatics bears some resemblance

---

[1] See Ch. 4, sect. 1(i).

to the types of relativity, in that it entails the non-absolute nature of the starting-points of all views.

Rorty's attack upon the traditional Philosophical[2] enterprise of epistemology is well known. He argues that the Philosophical concern with the foundations of knowledge 'is the product of the choice of perceptual metaphors'[3] which characterizes Western thought. The metaphor of our perception being the mirror of nature has been transformed from being a metaphor to a literal notion, resulting in the fruitless Philosophical search for a cogent correspondence theory of truth. Epistemology is a consequence of absolutizing a relative metaphor. 'To think of knowledge which presents a "problem" and about which we ought to have a "theory" is a product of viewing knowledge as an assemblage of representations—a view of knowledge which . . . was a product of the seventeenth century.'[4] Not only is Philosophy relative to a perceptual metaphor, but also that metaphor is outdated. Philosophy, and all the traditional tasks which it comprises, is not in error except in that it has failed to produce any useful results. 'Several hundred years of effort have failed to make interesting sense of the notion of correspondence.'[5]

Rorty replaces Philosophy with pragmatics. This way of thinking recognizes the contingency of all ways of looking at the world, and holds that contingency cannot be superseded. Accepting this fact, it is better, not to adopt theses or put forward arguments, but to give pictures, primarily of the history of thought, thus illustrating the bankruptcy of concepts and metaphors which simply have no life today outside of Philosophy journals. Rorty groups God and Philosophy together as words which simply no longer have any purchase upon Western, liberal intellectual life.

The most common criticisms of Rorty are that he has misrepresented the history of Philosophy, or at least what empiricists and rationalists are up to today, and that he has removed something which he has not come to terms with, namely the key notion of getting something right.[6] I, however, wish to offer the

---

[2] Rorty calls this Philosophy rather than philosophy, and I shall follow his convention in this section.

[3] Richard Rorty, *Philosophy and the Mirror of Nature* (Oxford: Basil Blackwell, 1980), 158.　　　　　　　　　　　　　　　　　　[4] Ibid. 136.

[5] Rorty, *Consequences of Pragmatism*, p. xvii.

[6] See e.g. Bernard Williams, 'Getting it Right', *London Review of Books* (23 Nov. 1989), 3–4.

opposite horn of this criticism, that Rorty has retained the very
notion of getting it right which he has striven to remove.

Rorty is another example of a thinker who must employ criteria in order to make judgements about what philosophy should
be. He accepts that there is rarely agreement over criteria, but
argues that for a pragmatist this should be expected. The pragmatist sees criteria as 'temporary resting-places constructed for
specific utilitarian ends'.[7] The 'vocabularies' (approximately
equivalent to some member of the list headed by 'conceptual
frameworks') which we employ, which include our criteria, are
judged by their utility. A good vocabulary is a useful one, and
this in practice appears to be one rightly used by a Western,
liberal intellectual. Bad vocabularies are those which have no
use, and have been shown by historical description to have no
use: such are the vocabularies of religion and Philosophy. These
vocabularies have no 'cash value', 'efficiency', 'utility', or 'profit-
ability'.[8] Therefore they should be discarded.

In this discussion, Rorty exhibits an infelicitous bifurcation
between his pragmatism and his own less pragmatic judgements.
Pragmatism, which on my broad typology of relativity looks
like a form of conceptual or epistemological relativism, rests
upon certain tenets which it takes as non-pragmatic: the unavoidability of contingency and the appropriateness of the criterion of
utility. The worry, as with any form of relativism, is how these
tenets prevent the original thesis from being self-referentially
incoherent. If all starting-points are contingent, then why is the
starting-point which recognizes this, namely pragmatism, not also
contingent? And if all methods of using criteria are contingent,
why is the criterion of utility not also contingent? If the starting-
point of pragmatism is contingent, then it is only to be adopted
by those who find it useful (against Rorty's own claims for it),
which makes it subject to conceptual relativity; and if the criterion of utility is contingent, then it is a criterion which others
can choose not to employ (again against Rorty's claims for it),
which makes it subject to epistemological relativity. Either Rorty's
pragmatism is incoherent, by not being contingent itself, or it is
contingent and is thus subject to the fact of relativity.

[7] Rorty, *Consequences of Pragmatism*, p. xli.
[8] All words used in the first chapter of Rorty, *Contingency, Irony and Solidarity*.

Rorty does not follow through the relativistic consequences of his pragmatism. For him, the old project of Philosophy has nothing left to say for itself; nor does religion, owing to the secularization of society. Rorty's tendency to make unacceptable generalizations such as these, and those about religion, without any extended support, gives the impression that he is replacing the old Philosophical attempt to discover the non-relative with a new, liberal outlook which takes its own thesis of pragmatism as resting upon a non-relatively useful vocabulary. Rorty concludes that religion no longer has cash value; whereas the consequence of pragmatism should only be that religion no longer has cash value for someone of a Western liberal stance of Rorty's kind.

Rorty approves of the line of thought in which 'we try to get to the point where we no longer worship *anything*, where we treat *nothing* as a quasi divinity, where we treat *everything*—our language, our conscience, our community—as a product of time and chance'.[9] What he is in effect doing is taking the sovereignty and authority of contingency as his non-relative position from which his contingent assertions can flow. Rorty cannot avoid what I shall describe as fundamental trust, even though his writing consistently suggests that he feels that he has.

What is interesting from a more positive angle is Rorty's distinction between normal and abnormal discourse. He defines them thus: 'Normal discourse is any discourse (scientific, political, theological, or whatever) which embodies agreed-upon criteria for reaching agreement; abnormal discourse is any which lacks such criteria.'[10] Epistemology—the enterprise of Philosophy— treats its issues as being in normal discourse. Philosophy assumes complete commensurability; in Rorty's words, being 'able to be brought under a set of rules which tell us how rational agreement can be reached on what would settle the issue on every point where statements seem to conflict'.[11] Pragmatics, on the other hand, prefers incommensurability, the possibility of conflict no longer being felt. This Rorty sometimes identifies with hermeneutics.[12]

Rorty's distinction hints at one which I wish to make concerning disagreement and disparity. Normal and abnormal discourse

---

[9] Ibid. 32.    [10] Rorty, *Philosophy and the Mirror of Nature*, 11.
[11] Ibid. 316.    [12] Ibid. 315.

will not quite do here, because they are limited to extremes. In normal discourse, there is complete commensurability: in other words, all criteria and language in normal discourse can be discussed, compared, and translated one to another. In abnormal discouse, this can never be done. No link exists to provide common understanding.

This distinction does not allow for most situations of discourse, conceptual frameworks, and so on, in which there are degrees of possible links and possible gaps in understanding and communication. If commensurability is kept to refer to complete translatability and sharing of criteria, as Rorty's notion of normal discourse suggests, and if incommensurability is the complete opposite, as Rorty's notion of abnormal discourse suggests, then this distinction cannot accept situations of some degree of common linkage, but not total linkage. Agreement and disagreement can occur with commensurability, as defined above, *or with a sufficiently common linkage of criteria, dispositions, or conceptual frameworks.* Disparity can occur with incommensurability, as defined above, *or with any lack of a sufficiently common linkage of criteria, dispositions, or conceptual frameworks.* Whether each situation is one of disagreement or disparity therefore needs to be given particular attention, since it may not be obvious what may comprise a 'sufficiently common linkage' in each case. Thus, I move on from the hint in Rorty's distinction between normal and abnormal discourse to a discussion of disagreement and disparity.

### (ii) *Disagreement and disparity*

These two concepts refer in slightly different ways to the types of relativity. Disagreement between conceptual frameworks requires sufficient common ground between them to allow at least the possibility of resolution. This is a common situation, at least within a single culture. My conceptual framework is inescapably different from yours—since we are different people—yet we can usually reach potential agreement over an issue: over whether A is taller than B, whether a tree is an oak or a beech, whether a hypothesis is well or badly supported by evidence.

Disparity of conceptual frameworks is more obvious between societies. If one society has the concept of snow, and another does not, and has no concepts to do with coldness at all, then there is little conceptual likelihood of understanding coldness between the societies. This is not the same as the dogmatic assertion of the incommensurability thesis (as I have understood it) that concepts cannot be translated from one conceptual framework to another. It is to say that on some occasions one conceptual framework will not be able to understand, respond to, or interact with a particular concept, or some particular concepts, of another conceptual framework. We have to learn Latin in order to gain an idea of what the word 'gloria' means; but to understand it properly we need an understanding of the place of this concept in Roman society. Traditionally Communist countries may not be able to grasp the concept of the free market; members of the artistic community may find quantum mechanics opaque; and so on.

Disagreement over preconceptual dispositions requires a sufficiently common linkage between the dispositions of different cultures or individuals. If there is empathy or sympathy between you and me in our feeling for nature, say, then we can disagree over particular features within that general feeling. With disparity, however, there is no such sufficiently common linkage. As there will be no empathy, or sufficient sympathy, over dispositions, individuals or societies will be unable to communicate or debate properly. One society might have a disposition toward women which another society feels is sexist; and if these dispositions do not link in a sufficient way, then there is a disparity of dispositions between these two societies.

Perhaps most interesting is the relation of disagreement and disparity to epistemological relativity. In the case of disagreement, there are common criteria, or extremely similar criteria, by which judgements can be made. If we want to confirm a scientific hypothesis, we perform an appropriate experiment; if we differ over what colour a species of flower is, we can check in a reference book or look at an actual example; if we differ over the merits of two political leaders, but agree that the better of the two is the one with the greater compassion, then at least theoretically we can decide which is the better political leader.

In the case of disparity, there are no shared or closely linked criteria. Imagine the issue of the role of classics (the study of Greek and Latin) in education. A government spokesman argues that classics should be largely removed from schools because it serves no purpose; in other words, it will not benefit the future adults of society. An opponent might argue that classics is inherently important, that considerations of utility are irrelevant. One is arguing using utility as a criterion, the other using inherent quality. The point is that the criteria being used are not similar, but quite disparate. No resolution of the debate is possible unless one of the criteria is radically altered. In my terminology, there is no disagreement here, only disparity, because there are no shared criteria which make it possible to agree or disagree.

My distinction is similar to that of Wittgenstein. For Wittgenstein, agreement and disagreement make sense within a language game, but clashes between forms of life, language games, or world pictures are not of this kind. They lie more deeply than agreement and disagreement, for in order to disagree one must have some criterion, disposition, or conceptual framework in common which provides the basis for disagreement.

However, the difference between clashes within a language game and disparity between language games is clearly brought out by Wittgenstein's examples of the Last Judgement and of seeing illness as a punishment. Wittgenstein argues that believing in the Last Judgement is not like believing that there is a German plane overhead. If I dispute the latter, then we are disagreeing, but if I dispute the former, there is 'an enormous gulf between us'.[13] We do not disagree; we simply differ over whether the picture of the Last Judgement plays a role in our lives. To say that we disagree is like saying that Aborigines disagree with modern science: rather, in one society or in one person a picture makes sense, and in another it does not.

The same is true for seeing illness as a punishment:

Suppose someone is ill and he says: 'This is a punishment', and I say: 'If I'm ill, I don't think of punishment at all.' If you say: 'Do you believe the opposite?'—you can call it believing the opposite, but it is entirely different from what we would normally call believing the opposite.

I think differently, in a different way. I say different things to myself. I have different pictures.

It is this way; if someone said: 'Wittgenstein, you don't take illness as a punishment, so what do you believe?'—I'd say: 'I don't have any thoughts of punishment.'[14]

[13] Wittgenstein, *Lectures and Conversations*, 53.     [14] Ibid. 55.

In my terminology, there is a situation of disparity between Wittgenstein and the believer in illness as a punishment. They simply do not share a sufficiently common picture to be said to disagree. In Chapter 6, I shall apply my distinction to the debate between Swinburne and Phillips over the appropriateness of the Proofs.

## 2. PERSONAL ABSOLUTES AND ABSOLUTES *PER SE*

The final distinction I wish to make before expounding my own conception of fundamental trust is that between absolutes *per se* and personal absolutes. I shall do this by following a distinction made by Joseph Runzo, one of the few thinkers to apply relativity in a positive way to the question of religious belief.

### (i) *The absolute in Christianity*

In his book *Reason, Relativism and God*,[15] Runzo accepts the unavoidability of conceptual and epistemological relativity and attempts to reconcile this with the inherently absolutist claims of traditional Christianity. He identifies three possible candidates for the absolutist element of Christian faith which is intended to overcome relativity.

The first is religious experience. The idea of Schleiermacher, Buber, and others is that an experience of God can provide absolute knowledge. Runzo rejects this on the grounds that all knowledge is relative to a conceptual schema. Our experience cannot go beyond the structure made possible by our own already existing conceptual framework. All knowledge is relative to one's conceptual schema, and this is true even of knowledge acquired through religious experience.

Secondly, metaphysics is intended to overcome relativity. Traditionally, metaphysics has been conceived as an attempt by the human mind to discover the truth, truth of an absolute kind. Bultmann was right in arguing against Barth that all theology has metaphysical presuppositions, whether conscious or unconscious, and thus theology is often thought of as perceiving the

---

[15] Runzo, *Reason, Relativism and God*. All references in this section will be to this book.

truth about God. However, no presuppositions are neutral, for they are all relative to the conceptual framework of the presupposer. This is true of metaphysical presuppositions as well as any other. Thus the theologian's conception of God must be recognized as his own, relative conception which might be wrong. It might be wrong—and, therefore, equally it might be right—because the fact of relativity is itself relative. By its own logic, the fact of relativity allows for the *possibility* of an accurate non-relative conception. Metaphysics cannot overcome relativity because 'a relativistic epistemology will have logical priority for theology over an absolutist metaphysics' (p. 137).

Thirdly, the central New Testament message of proclamation, the *kerygma*, is intended to overcome relativity. Bultmann and Barth both hold that Christianity, with its claim to the absolute, is beyond the relativistic situation of world views. However, they are wrong, since any individual's reaction to the *kerygma* will be relative to that individual's conceptual framework, and 'proclamation can only come to humans in human language, using human concepts with all their historical and cultural relativity' (p. 166).

However, for Runzo, there is a sense in which faith in the *kerygma* is absolute. To see this it is necessary to distinguish between two kinds of absolute: the absolute *per se* and the personal absolute. The former is absolute for any conceptual framework whatever: an example for Runzo would be the law of non-contradiction. The latter refers to a truth which is absolute within a particular schema; in other words, some tenets must be 'treated as absolute on the grounds that the relative truth to which they refer cannot be given up without literally annihilating the schema in which they are embedded' (p. 155). Such truths are absolute from the relative perspective of the person who holds them to be true.

Runzo argues that faith in the *kerygma* is absolute relative not to any conceptual framework at all but to any which can make sense of and respond to the *kerygma*. The proclamation is absolute relative to Christianity, but not absolute *per se*. To suppose otherwise is to absolutize a human reaction, or human language, whereas any response to or words about God must be seen as relative. The only absolute standard is God. It is a matter of trust that Christians suppose their own conception of God somehow to refer to the real, absolute God.

## (ii) *Absolutes and trust*

While not wishing to agree with all of Runzo's account, I do think that it reveals another important element of a discussion of relativity: namely, that of trust. Runzo correctly sees that, on some conceptions of God, there is no guarantee of man's conception of God being an accurate one (although the possibility that it is accurate is still there): much as from many philosophical perspectives, there is no guarantee that man's conception of the external world, of other minds, and so on is accurate. From these perspectives, any belief in God, the world, and other people rests upon trust, a trust that there is some correlation between God etc. and one's own personal belief. Such a trust, if it forms the deepest and most integral part of one's conceptual framework, I term fundamental trust.

It is worth noting briefly that fundamental trust is ineluctable. It takes different forms from different perspectives, but since (if my discussion is correct) no fundamental presupposition can be fully justified, without at least relying unquestioningly upon another such presupposition (the lesson of Neurath's ship), there must be a fundamental trust in some part of, or totality of, a way of looking at the world, in some of one's dispositions, and in some of one's criteria for making judgements.

We can thus see how conceptual, preconceptual, and epistemological relativity need not be the end of the story. To be aware of the relativity of conceptual frameworks, dispositions, and criteria for making judgements does not involve a particular attitude toward such relativity. One may see this situation as the end of the matter, exhibiting a fundamental trust in contingency or relativity (thus Rorty exhibits a fundamental trust within his philosophy in contingency being the last word); or one may say that relativity cannot be the end, because complete relativity is incoherent (a fundamental trust in the law of non-contradiction), or because relativity is transcended in some way (a fundamental trust in the transcendent).

Runzo exhibits fundamental trust in the truth of conceptual relativity. He uses this to deny the possibility of using religious experience or metaphysics as a grounding for absolute truth. Note here the truth of Runzo's own observation that some things must be held as non-relative, for this is certainly how he views the truth of conceptual relativity. This is not something to be eschewed, as long as one is aware of the situation, for it seems impossible to hold all one's beliefs, make all one's claims to truth, and adopt all one's criteria relatively: for this in itself is to treat relativity as non-relative, as something which is true above and beyond particular situations.

It is noteworthy further that Runzo holds the law of non-contradiction non-relatively. It is intended to apply to all conceptual schemas, and this is a view often held within philosophy. Yet it is important to see that to treat such a principle as non-relative is itself an example of trust: for many thinkers, particularly of a mystical turn, paradox and contradiction are simply unavoidable and indeed appropriate in talk about that which transcends human categories, such as God.

Absolutes *per se* are seemingly impossible for human beings. All of our absolutes appear to be related to particular frameworks, attitudes, and sets of criteria. Yet to assert non-relatively that there could never be an absolute *per se*, or that it could never impinge upon human life, is to assert the fact of relativity absolutely. To avoid doing this, it is necessary to remember and emphasize the essential role of trust in dealing with the absolute and the relative. It is this task which I shall perform in the next section.

## 3. THE CONCEPT OF FUNDAMENTAL TRUST

It is difficult to see initially how the concept of fundamental trust is related to relativism. For genuine relativism, as I have discussed it, all views are relative except relativism itself. Thus relativism can be *known* to be true. We do not have to trust in the thesis of relativism, for it can be a subject of knowledge for us.

I shall argue later that, despite this superficial appearance, relativism, and, indeed, any theory, framework, attitude, or set of criteria, is based upon trust. It is most clear, however, how trust relates to the fact of relativity. This fact cannot definitely be taken to be known to be absolute or to be relative. Taking it to be absolute goes against the fact of relativity by making it an exception to the fact itself, while taking it as relative eliminates, in a non-relative manner, the possibility of some dissolution or transcendence of relativity. Hence trust is involved in how one interprets the fact of relativity, since relativity cannot, by its own logic, be taken to be definitely absolute or definitely relative.

In this section I will attempt four things. In (i) I will discuss what I take to be the relevant characteristics of trust for my discussion, without expecting complete consensus on these characteristics and without intending to give an exhaustive characterization of trust. In (ii) I will contrast trust with fundamental trust, illustrating how the latter applies to all the listed types of relativity. To avoid confusion of fundamental trust with two similar and popular concepts, I shall contrast it in (iii) with Plantinga's 'basic beliefs' and in (iv) with Wittgenstein's 'groundless beliefs'.

## (i) *Trust*

The following characteristics of trust I take to be relevant to the discussion of the appropriateness of the Proofs, as I shall argue in the next chapter, and to provide a part of a relatively adequate account of trust generally.

(*a*) *Trust is inescapable.*   Everyone trusts something. In our everyday life we trust that when we put our foot on to the ground, the ground will hold us up and not subside. We trust that when we go outside, we will be able to breathe in the air. We trust that as the sun has risen every day of our lives so it will rise tomorrow.

These examples of trust share the common characteristic of being tacit or unconscious for most people for most of the time. When we put our foot on a pavement, and the pavement holds us up, we do not ordinarily think: 'My trust in the solidity of the pavement has been proved correct in this instance; I hope it proves correct in the next instance as well.' (Although, of course, it would be unsurprising if this were thought by someone who was living in San Francisco at a time when an earthquake was forecast.)

The unconscious nature of such trust is a consequence of its inescapability and pervasiveness. Human beings could not function without generally trusting in the evidence of their senses, in the time given by clocks and watches, in the solidity of objects, and so on. As Niklas Luhmann writes about anyone, 'a complete absence of trust would prevent him from getting up in the morning'.[16]

---

[16] Niklas Luhmann, *Trust and Power*, trans. Howard Davies *et al.* (Chichester: John Wiley and Sons, 1979), 4.

(*b*) *Trust reflects uncertainty.* If we know *x*, then it seems to make little sense to say that we trust that *x*. This reflects the fact that we normally speak about trust in situations in which complete certainty is not possible. I know that 2 + 2 = 4, but I trust that the sun will be out at the weekend.

Wolfhart Pannenberg has characterized this element of trust particularly well. He writes that 'Trust is a constant necessity in daily life. Wherever man has to be involved with things and forces whose inner nature is not completely transparent, trust is unavoidable.'[17] Reality is not transparent to us: things can always turn out differently from the way in which we expected them to. Trust is essential in situations of uncertainty, and as 'the reality on the strength of which we live always remains unknown',[18] trust occurs pervasively.

(*c*) *Trust involves risk.* It is a further consequence of the fact that trust is found in situations of uncertainty that trust involves risk. If we cannot be certain that the rope will not break, then it is a risk to trust it by using it. If we cannot be certain that another person will be loyal, then trust in their friendship is a risk. In the face of relativity, we cannot be certain in such situations; hence the pervasiveness of trust and the risk it entails. It is always possible that one's trust is misplaced, irrelevant, inadequate. One could be wrong in any situation, since even 'being certain' and 'knowing' are dependent upon frameworks and criteria which we can only trust, as I will argue under (*f*).

(*d*) *Trust involves action.* If I trust that the world is a good place then my actions will consequently be of a certain kind. If I trust people as being inherently good and kind, then my actions will be of a more pleasant nature than if I did not so trust. One cannot avoid the sphere of acting (even inaction is involved in this sphere, as the negative of acting), because everyone is in an existential situation to which they respond, both consciously and unconsciously. Owing to the pervasiveness of situations of uncertainty, and the inescapability of acting in response to such situations, one's trust in what is true or likely or appropriate results in action.

[17] Wolfhart Pannenberg, *What is Man?*, trans. Duane A. Priebe (Philadelphia: Fortress Press, 1970), 30.                                        [18] Ibid. 29.

(e) *Trust is predictive.* If I trust in the reliability of a friend, then I make a prediction about how that friend will behave in the future. If I trust in the strength of a rope to get me across a stream, then I am making a prediction about the rope and what will happen when I use it. Trust thus involves a predictive element.

Such predictions are based on trust and not certainty or knowledge, because of the fact of relativity. I think that the rope will get me across the stream, but this can only be trust because I cannot be sure. I think that my friend is reliable, but this can only be trust because there is always a possibility that he or she will prove unreliable in the future. Not only does trust involve prediction, but the very prediction itself relies upon trust.

(f) *Trust has an object.* If I trust, then I must trust in something or someone, or that something. I can trust in my parents, the solidity of the ground, the power of politics, the beauty of the countryside. I can trust that the world powers are committed to peace, there is a country called Australia, all swans are white or black. Trust can also have as its object any of the subjects of the types of relativity listed earlier: one can trust in a particular world view, in intuition, in the authority of a particular criterion. These types of trust, which are especially important for my discussion, I will discuss more fully under fundamental trust.

(g) *Trust is relative.* The fact of relativity applies as much to trust as to any other concept or phenomenon. The objects of my trust will be different from yours, regardless of any similarities. People trust in a variety of different things, and at a variety of different levels. Trust can be in particulars, like the strength of a rope or the reliability of a friend; in universals, like the goodness of religion or the impotence of politics; or in methods of judgement, such as empirical testing or rational justification.

H. Richard Niebuhr, whose important work on the relative and the absolute I shall consider in a little more detail in the next section, makes the point well, referring to faith rather than trust. 'No man lives without living for some purpose, for the glorification of some god, for the advancement of some cause. . . . The private faith by which we live is likely to be a multifarious thing with many objects of devotion and worship.'[19]

## (ii) *Fundamental trust*

I now wish to distinguish trust from what I shall call fundamental trust. The distinction here rests upon the depth or priority of the trust in question. The deepest kind of trust, in terms of importance and place in the epistemological order, is fundamental trust. Its priority lies in it being the part of a person's make-up which is not founded upon anything else. It is the bottom line beyond which it makes no sense to go.

When a person's trust alters, the person too alters, but not necessarily in a deep or major way. However, when a person's fundamental trust alters, then there is a substantial upheaval in that person. A whole way of looking at things, an entire attitude, a method of making judgements, has become obsolete or untrustworthy for that person. The altering of something fundamental to a person will entail the deepest possible change in the person concerned.

Fundamental trust need not be monistic, although it can be. Some people might have fundamental trust in God, or in reason, or in life. Generally, however, people will have a variety of objects of fundamental trust: the evidence of our senses, learning from experience, the evidence of our memory, and the existence of an external world might all be objects of fundamental trust for a deeply rooted empiricist. It is highly plausible to suppose that psychological and sociological forces will have some influence over what one trusts fundamentally; but to suppose that they fully explain this is simply to assert one's fundamental trust in the reductive power of psychological and sociological explanation.

I shall now attempt to elucidate the distinction between trust and fundamental trust further by relating them to the four types of relativity which I outlined in the last chapter.

(*a*) *Conceptual relativity.* Fundamental trust in a conceptual framework occurs when the framework lies at the heart of a

---

[19] H. Richard Niebuhr, *Radical Monotheism and Western Culture* (London: Faber and Faber, 1943), 118–19.

person's or society's make-up. It is a framework which lies below the level of justification, and below other frameworks which are only trusted in.

An example of a fundamental trust with regard to cognitive relativity would be in a religious conceptual framework for an utterly devoted believer. All of life is related to this person's understanding of religion, and everything outside of religion is seen through the religious conceptual framework. The framework itself is not subsequent to any other framework trusted in by this person; it is the ultimate framework through which all else is related.

An example of cultural relativity would be in the power of drugs for the society of Huxley's *Brave New World*. In this society, drugs are taken regularly and affect the society's perspective upon all else it experiences. The framework of the drug-centred world view is trusted in fundamentally by this society.

One can see how two fundamental trusts could easily lead to disparity within conceptual relativity. If I trust in Communism as the fundamentally apposite world view, and you trust fundamentally in some traditional form of Christianity, then disparity between our fundamental trusts seems inevitable. If, however, there is a sufficiently common link between our fundamental trusts, say (perhaps) between a Christian and a Jewish world view, then there would be disagreement rather than disparity.

*(b) Preconceptual relativity.* It is important to distinguish fundamental trust itself from what is constituted by preconceptual relativity. There can be fundamental trust in any preconceptual element such as intuition, disposition, or insight. An example of such fundamental trust would be in love as a panacea, or as an undergirding of all life. One could even have a fundamental trust in trust, seeing trust as the basic human relationship, or the attitude which everyone should most try to cultivate.

However, fundamental trust itself does not fit so snugly into the category of preconceptual relativity. Rather, the concept of preconceptual relativity is designed to refer to those attitudes, dispositions, and so on which might be the objects of fundamental trust. I shall defer discussion of the relativity of fundamental trust to the fourth type of relativity.

It is easy to see how two fundamental trusts in elements of

preconceptual relativity could lead to disagreement or disparity. Disagreement could be reached by having fundamental trusts in, respectively, love and hate. There is a common link in that fundamental trusts are in emotions, and there is disagreement over which emotion should be the object of fundamental trust. Disparity occurs in a situation in which fundamental trusts share insufficiently common links, such as in love and in intuition.

(c) *Epistemological relativity*.  Fundamental trust in the case of epistemological relativity is in the most central and integral criteria for making judgements. It is in criteria which determine what we count as our most basic concepts, such as truth, knowledge, and rationality.

It applies to both internal and external relativism. For the former, imagine two people who accept the integrity of Bill Clinton, and that a case is made against him that he was involved in bribery. The first person accepts the case—'the evidence convinced me'. The second person does not accept the case, not because he finds the evidence unconvincing, but because 'Clinton is just not that sort of man'. The first person might call the second stubborn; but all this means is that the two people do not share the same criteria for judging the allegation. The first person is more committed to the evidence of his senses than to Clinton's integrity; the second person, if he really means that no grounds would count against Clinton's integrity, has fundamental trust in Clinton's integrity. Similarly, if the first person really held that we ought always to accept the evidence of our senses, then he would have fundamental trust in our senses.

For the latter, imagine two Christian denominations, one which judges the truth of Christian teaching on the basis of the Bible as the ultimate source of authority, and one which uses the Pope as the ultimate source of authority. One has fundamental trust in the authority of the Bible, the other has fundamental trust in the Pope.

Again, it is easy to see how differences in trusts can lead to disagreement or disparity. If it is agreed that we can fundamentally trust in the evidence of our senses as a criterion for making judgements about the composition of the external world, but one person or school fundamentally trusts in sight above the other senses, and another person or school fundamentally trusts in touch above the other senses, then there is a sufficiently shared fundamental trust for there to be disagreement. If, however, as in the case of the Bible or the Pope being the ultimate criterion of authority for religious truth, there is no sufficiently common link, then we have a case of disparity of fundamental trusts. This last case also clearly reveals the vital point that there can be a disparity of fundamental trusts over a single, shared issue. The single issue here is the ultimate criterion for judging the truth of religious claims; yet the different fundamental trusts in what such a criterion should be have insufficiently common links and are therefore disparate. This point will be important in my discussion of the difference between Swinburne and Phillips over the appropriateness of the Proofs.

We can see the role of fundamental trust in elements of epistemological relativity in the work of Dilthey and Kaufman. Dilthey has a fundamental trust in *Erlebnis* being the ultimate criterion for making judgements, while Kaufman has a fundamental trust in the noumenal God being the ultimate criterion for making religious judgements. The relativity of epistemological criteria reveals the relativity of their own objects of fundamental trust.

(*d*) *Surface and depth relativity.* These types of relativity refer to the distinction between conceptual and epistemological relativity. Surface relativity occurs when the issue of divergence is a matter of fact or truth or piece of knowledge. Depth relativity, however, occurs when what it is to count as a fact or as truth or as a piece of knowledge is the subject of divergence. The importance of this distinction will be made clearer when it is applied to the debate between Swinburne and Phillips in the next chapter.

The important issue which we are left with concerns the relativity of fundamental trust. The objects of fundamental trust have been seen to be subject to the types of relativity which I have outlined, and it appears that the same thing is true of fundamental trust itself. There is a relativity of fundamental trusts as there is a relativity of other trusts; the difference is that the relativity applies at the level which it makes no sense to go beyond. If relativity affects fundamental trust, then human beings and whole societies have to face up to the relativity of the most deep-rooted and integral parts of their lives.

The difficulty of accepting such a situation is well expressed by H. Richard Niebuhr, who is quite aware of the human tendency to absolutize the relative. He writes of man's 'unconquerable tendency to absolutise some relative starting-point such as man, or ideas, or life'.[20] Niebuhr is concerned to keep the relative and the absolute strictly apart in the face of this tendency. Relative starting-points must be accepted as relative, and not confused with what Niebuhr calls the transcendent absolute. He warns us against 'the dogmatism of a relativism which assumes the privileged position of one finite reality, such as man'.[21]

The transcendent absolute is God. Only God is absolute, and it is idolatrous to take anything finite, such as a human conception of God, as absolute. In the face of the fact of relativity, Niebuhr commends radical monotheism, which reveres the relative for being relative and worships only the Absolute as absolute. This absolute, *pace* Tillich, appears to reside in Being. 'For radical monotheism the value-center is neither closed society nor the principle of such a society but the principle of being itself; its reference is to no one reality among the many but to One beyond all the many, whence all the many derive their being, and by participation in which they exist.'[22]

The worry with Niebuhr's account is how, in the face of the fact of relativity, this absolute is possible, discernible by human beings, or characterizable. If all characteristics of the Absolute are relative, then this applies to such labels as 'being' and 'God' as much as to any other; and if a characterization of the Absolute is not relative, then somehow Niebuhr has done what on his account seems impossible, and, as a human being, transcended the fact of relativity.

The great merit of Niebuhr's account, it seems to me, is twofold. First, it reminds us of the relative character of our absolutes. This fits in with Runzo's description of personal absolutes, absolutes which are relative to a particular, relative framework, disposition, or set of criteria. The objects of fundamental trust are taken to be non-relative by almost everyone, but Niebuhr and Runzo remind us that such objects are not necessarily absolutes *per se*; rather, we take them as absolutes. The fact of relativity imbues the human situation with an ambiguity. It suggests that

[20] Ibid. 111–12.    [21] Ibid. 112.    [22] Ibid. 32.

objects of fundamental trust can only be taken *as* non-relative, not *that they are* non-relative; and yet the fact of relativity does not permit us to assert the above point in a non-relative way. It is opposed to the fact of relativity to assert that objects of fundamental trust can only be taken *as* absolutes, for this assertion is itself relative. Perhaps some personal absolutes are absolutes *per se*.

Hence, secondly, we can see the importance of Niebuhr's attempt to posit an absolute beyond the confines of relativity. While I have argued that his characterization of the absolute is itself relative, it is important to see that genuine appreciation of the relativity of the fact of relativity makes it impossible to rule out the possibility of an absolute beyond relativity. This is partly why it is so valuable to examine the writings of thinkers who have considered relativity and attempted to go beyond it.

Once again we return to the issue of whether fundamental trust and its objects are relative. One can now see, I think, by learning from Niebuhr and Runzo, that there is an inescapable tension between the relativity, and the non-relativity, of fundamental trust. The fact of relativity suggests that even at the most fundamental level, our frameworks, dispositions, and criteria are relative; and yet the relativity of this statement suggests that, possibly, our fundamental trusts and their objects are not relative. This is an inescapable tension which follows from my own, relative discussion of relativity.

In the next chapter I will apply the conclusions of this chapter and the last to the question of the appropriateness of the Proofs, and the way in which the fact of relativity impinges upon the way in which we interpret the Proofs themselves. In the remainder of this chapter, however, I will distinguish my conception of fundamental trust from two popular and speciously similar conceptions, basic belief and groundless belief.

### (iii) *Basic belief*

The single most important expositor of reformed epistemology, the label given to the movement concerned with basic belief, is Alvin Plantinga, and it is his writings which I shall concentrate on.

A basic belief is one not held on the basis of other beliefs or propositions, and one that need not rely upon any supporting argument.[23] A *properly* basic belief is one held fast by circumstances which rationally justify that belief. Basic beliefs, then, are not groundless, as they are for Wittgenstein, because they are held in place by the circumstances which produce them. If I believe in God by experiencing the starry heavens, and Calvin is right that the starry heavens are a proper phenomenon to produce belief in God, then my belief in God is properly basic.

Plantinga's task is one of negative apologetics: to show that belief in God speaking to me, for example,[24] is as properly basic as many secular beliefs. Plantinga is not concerned to provide a criterion of basicality—indeed, he counts all the criteria as yet provided, by classical foundationalism[25] and by Alston and Kenny,[26] as self-referentially incoherent—yet he does not hold that the search for such a criterion is senseless.

This illustrates that in Plantinga's picture of the human noetic structure, basic belief (unlike fundamental trust) is not the bottom level. It makes sense to search for a deeper criterion which grounds a basic belief, while it makes no sense to look for such a criterion to justify fundamental trust. One cannot say that one has some cogent non-propositional evidence for one's fundamental trust in $x$, for then one's fundamental trust would be in the criterion and not in $x$. It makes no sense to look for a criterion to justify fundamental trust.

Plantinga is clearly concerned to distinguish basic belief from groundless belief. He is worried, in his reply to the Great Pumpkin objection (that if we can provide no criterion for properly basic belief, then any belief—such as belief in the Great Pumpkin—is as good as any other), that his account of belief makes belief gratuitous. He insists that to say that beliefs are properly

[23] Alvin Plantinga, 'The Reformed Objection to Natural Theology', in *Proceedings of The American Catholic Association*, 1980, p. 53. The account I give of reformed epistemology has to be gleaned from Plantinga's several similar papers on the same subject: see bibliography.

[24] Belief in God is not properly basic, because it is subsequent to other beliefs, such as belief in God speaking to me. I shall argue later in this section that this is a problem within Plantinga's position.

[25] The theory that a basic belief is properly basic if and only if it is self-evident, incorrigible, or evident to the senses.

[26] See Plantinga, 'On Our Knowing God', the unpublished Wilde Lectures given at Oxford University, Trinity Term, 1988.

basic 'is not to deny that there are justifying conditions for these beliefs, or conditions that confer justification on one who accepts them as basic. They are therefore not groundless or gratuitous.'[27] It is noteworthy how easily the term 'groundless', which has its own respected philosophical heritage, is so easily linked with the pejorative term 'gratuitous'. Plantinga's desire for basic belief to have a grounding illustrates its quite different role from that of fundamental trust. Thus my view is quite divergent from Plantinga's.

It is perhaps a disturbing consequence of Plantinga's reformed epistemology and its reliance upon circumstances which produce belief, that trust in God can never be more fundamental than trust in something more particular about God. This means that a belief in God which accepts the mysteriousness of God's nature and attributes cannot be acceptable on Plantinga's view, because one must be aware of something particular about God in order to have a general belief in God's reality. It is a worry that if Plantinga is right, no one could properly trust in God in a more fundamental way than trusting in a vision of God, for example. Plantinga's insistence upon circumstances undergirding belief, then, seems to be either an empirically testable hypothesis (which the above example of belief in God would seem to counter) or simply a relative expression of his own fundamental trust. This is why Phillips can write that 'Plantinga is still in the grip of the very foundationalism that he sets out to criticise'.[28]

## (iv) *Groundless belief*

It may appear that I have relied heavily upon some of Wittgenstein's thinking in this book (the difference between disparity and disagreement, the lack of a common language in which decisions can be made or common criteria with which to make decisions), thus prejudicing my account in favour of Phillips and against traditional philosophy of religion. In this section I wish to argue that this is not so by showing how my central notion of fundamental trust is different from Wittgenstein's conception of the groundlessness of belief. In this piece I shall unavoidably

[27] Alvin Plantinga, 'Is Belief in God Properly Basic?', *Nous*, 15 (1981), 48.
[28] Phillips, *Faith after Foundationalism*, 29.

be repeating some of Wittgenstein's ideas discussed in earlier chapters.

Wittgenstein's point that belief is ultimately groundless is quite simple to make but very difficult to grasp. His idea is that we ultimately reach a position in relation to certain beliefs where testing the belief makes no sense. The very notion of justifying or testing or doubting already presupposes that there is something that we do not test or doubt or need to justify. 'Whenever we test anything we are already presupposing something that is not tested.'[29] We have to presuppose a measure by which we measure other things. To doubt everything or hold everything in need of justification is impossible in practice.

This means that we must 'realise the groundlessness of our believing' (*OC* 166). At some point we reach a position in which it makes no sense to talk of grounds at all. We have to accept that, for example, our system of calculation is an appropriate one. If someone asked us to ground the system of calculation in which 2 + 2 = 4, we could not do it. The question really makes no sense. 'Somewhere we must be finished with justification, and then there remains the proposition that *this* is how we calculate' (*OC* 212). Another example would be induction. Hume showed up the inherent circularity of accepting induction; Wittgenstein says that belief in induction is therefore groundless. There is no possible non-circular ground that we could appeal to in order to justify our belief in induction.

This means that there is something ungrounded in all our thinking. It is 'something that lies beyond being justified or unjustified; as it were, something animal' (*OC* 359). Sometimes Wittgenstein calls this 'something' a language game,[30] at other times a world picture;[31] but on the most consistent reading of Wittgenstein, this something is a form of life. 'The end is not an ungrounded presupposition: it is an ungrounded way of acting' (*OC* 110). It is neither a way of seeing the world nor accordance with reality, neither the language one is involved in nor simply experience, that is fundamental: it is the circumstances which hold all these things together, and those circumstances are the

[29] Wittgenstein, *On Certainty*, 163. Future references to this work, abbreviated to *OC*, will be found in the text.
[30] e.g. *OC* 559, *Philosophical Investigations*, 656.          [31] e.g. *OC* 94, 146, 162.

ways in which we act and behave. 'What stands fast does so, not because it is intrinsically obvious or convincing; it is rather held fast by what lies around it' (*OC* 144).

There is certainly a close affinity between my own position and that of Wittgenstein. Indeed, Wittgenstein writes that 'I really want to say that a language game is only possible if one *trusts* something' (*OC* 509, my emphasis); and elsewhere that 'there seem to be propositions that have the character of existential propositions, but whose truth is for me unassailable. That is to say, if I assume that they are false, I must *mistrust* all my judgments.'[32] Wittgenstein might hold that trust and mistrust are deeper for us than knowledge, judgement, and language; but equally trust here is subordinate to the ways of acting that provide the context in which trust can be given.

This can be brought out by looking at Wittgenstein's comparison of trust and knowledge. Wittgenstein wants to hold that there is no *practical* difference between someone who knows that *x* and someone who only trusts that *x*. If I trust that the pavement will hold me up, how am I different in practice from the person who knows that the pavement holds me up? Wittgenstein answers that there is no difference.

I wish to argue that, while there may be no practical difference in this case, there can be practical differences in other similar cases. For example, consider a person who holds that because of some primal misdemeanour (Adam and Eve, perhaps) man is under sin in this world, but that there is a better place where man will not be under sin (Paradise or the Kingdom of God, perhaps). Now, this person behaves like Wittgenstein when she steps on to the pavement; but, unlike Wittgenstein, she is prepared to accept that our perceptions are faulty, that there is or could be a future life in which the possibility of mistakes is ruled out. In this person there is a quality of openness and unconditional rejection of the transitory that is notably lacking in Wittgenstein, and in Wittgenstein's conception of religion.

Similarly, if someone came to believe that this world was the work of the Devil, or that we were controlled by experimenters and had lost sight of our real humanity (as occurs in *1984* and

---

[32] Wittgenstein, *Remarks on Colour*, trans. Linda McAlister and Margaret Schattle (Oxford: Basil Blackwell, 1951), 348 (my emphasis).

*Brave New World*), they would have no reason to accept Wittgenstein's view that we are limited by our ways of acting. This is a point at which my conception of fundamental trust and Wittgenstein's conception of groundless belief sharply diverge. I wish to say that a person could have a fundamental trust which made him or her doubt the reality and reliability of this world, in favour of a transcendent certainty. This trust could infect that person's way of acting. Consider a holy man with such a trust; he would thoroughly merit the appellation 'holy' (which originally meant 'set apart'). He would not be involved in one of the shared ways of acting that Wittgenstein finds inviolable.

For Wittgenstein, the command is to 'forget this transcendent certainty, which is connected with your concept of spirit' (*OC* 47). Our certainty is entirely limited to our ways of acting. It is Wittgenstein's limiting that causes him to answer the following question in the negative: 'But might it not be possible for something to happen that threw me entirely off the rails? Evidence that made the most certain thing unacceptable to me? Or at any rate made me throw over my most fundamental judgments?' (*OC* 517)

This does not seem plausible for all viewpoints, however. Wittgenstein ignores the fact of relativity in his description. Aquinas, for example, having spent his life in the pursuit of natural knowledge of God, suddenly at the end of his life reviled the whole enterprise. He told his friend Reginald of Piperno: 'Reginald, I can write no more. . . . All that I have hitherto written seems to me nothing . . . compared to what I have seen and what has been revealed to me.'[33] Aquinas gave up his most fundamental certainties which stemmed from his practices. Wittgenstein's refusal to allow anything beyond the beliefs derived from our ways of acting causes him to deny transcendence to God. Talk of a transcendent God is simply nonsense.[34]

[33] Josef Pieper, *The Silence of St Thomas*, trans. Daniel O'Connor (London: Faber and Faber, 1957).

[34] There are passages in *On Certainty*, however, which conflict with this (traditional) picture of how Wittgenstein conceives of God; see *OC* 436, 578, 623. I would explain this by recalling that *On Certainty* is a collection of notes made by Wittgenstein for himself only; contradictions are consequently bound to occur. I suspect (though it is only a suspicion) that they reflect a tension in Wittgenstein himself between acceptance and rejection of God; a tension amply illustrated in accounts of Wittgenstein by his contemporaries.

I would suggest that Wittgenstein's argument reveals his fundamental trust in the limiting power of our ways of acting. He traps God within human conceptions of God. Our conceptions of God within our ways of acting are equated in practice with God's reality. There is no God beyond the religious language game for Wittgenstein; and this is partly the consequence of making ways of acting fundamental rather than trust. If ways of acting are fundamental, then anything like traditional theism or life after death is rendered impossible. If trust, however, is made fundamental, then such possibilities become what they actually are for some human beings; namely, possibilities. Wittgenstein has gone beyond his own motive of saying what people do and do not think, and has moved on to saying what people can and cannot think (for example, that people cannot think metaphysically). In this I suggest that I am closer than Wittgenstein to his own model of philosophy, namely pure description. Wittgenstein's refusal to accept the possibility of going beyond our practices is itself a reflection of his fundamental trust. I shall show how this fundamental trust has passed down to Phillips's way of thinking in the next chapter.

# 6

# The Appropriateness of the Proofs

In this final chapter, I wish to apply the conclusions of the previous two chapters to the issue between Swinburne and Phillips over the appropriateness of the Proofs of the existence of God. I will argue in the first section that the replies of Swinburne and Phillips to the fact of relativity are inadequate, and in the second section I will show how the three principles, or rejection of these principles, underlying their philosophies of religion reveal a situation of disparate fundamental trusts. I will argue further in the second section that, because of this disparity, there is no possibility of resolution over the appropriateness of the Proofs if one is limited to the positions of Swinburne and Phillips. Finally, in Section 3, I will describe how the fact of relativity infects interpretations of the Proofs themselves, giving the ontological argument as a detailed example, before drawing my conclusions in Section 4.

## 1. PHILOSOPHICAL RESPONSE TO RELATIVITY

The burden of my argument in Section 2 will be that the disparity between Swinburne and Phillips over the Proofs follows from the relativity of the philosophical and theological objects of their fundamental trusts. In this section, however, I wish to show that, despite an implicit response in Swinburne and an explicit response in Phillips, the fact of relativity is inescapable for each of them.

Although I am not aware of Swinburne writing explicitly on the subject of relativity, I think that it is possible to discover a tacit rejection of the pervasiveness of the fact of relativity. This rests in the underlying figure in Swinburne's work of *the* rational person. On several occasions, Swinburne refers to the hope that almost any rational person should be convinced by a particular argument, and sometimes he will accept that an argument can be sufficiently cogent to convince every rational person. This is true of his definition of the Christian God,[1] and of his defence of the coherence of theism.[2] The implication is that there is a paradigm standard of rationality to which people should adhere. Some arguments and claims adhere to this standard, and therefore should be assented to by any rational person.

This picture of rationality is denied not only by the Wittgensteinian school of philosophy, but also by the logic of the fact of relativity. Conceptual relativity does not allow for a definite, standard conception of rationality common to all frameworks. Even the law of non-contradiction need not be taken as non-relative.[3] Preconceptual relativity does not apply here, but epistemological relativity shows that it cannot be definitely asserted that there is a common set of criteria which can be used to judge what rationality is. What counts as comprising rationality for a present-day, Oxford philosopher heavily influenced by medieval canons of rationality cannot be taken, non-relatively, to be what counts as rationality for all situations and for all people (not even for all philosophers). The idea of arguments that any rational person should accept assumes not just the possibility of, but the actuality of, a single definitive criterion of rationality: and this the fact of relativity cannot allow.

What makes an acceptance of the fact of relativity superior to Swinburne's conception of the rational person is that it allows for, indeed feeds upon, the unquestionable multiplicity of points of view, sets of criteria, and so on. The logic of Swinburne's position is that all viewpoints other than his own are inadequate, because clearly he is aware of what actually does constitute reality. Our choice of what should count as rational depends upon our conceptual frameworks and criteria for making judgements, whether we are taken as individuals or societies, and therefore any conception of *the* rational person can only collapse into at least partly personal or social preference. Thus Swinburne's tacit response to the fact of relativity will not do.

Phillips's riposte to relativity is, I think, more subtle and

---

[1] Swinburne, *The Coherence of Theism*, preface.
[2] Swinburne, *The Existence of God*, introduction.
[3] See Ch. 5, sect. 2(ii).

challenging than Swinburne's. He in effect opposes the sense and content of the fact of relativity. Adopting Wittgenstein's framework, Phillips argues that right and wrong, and truth and falsity, only make sense within a language game or form of life. The practice itself, whether of religion or philosophy, cannot be right or wrong, because it is below the level at which right and wrong make sense. Since relativity is a description of claims to or criteria of truth and falsity, it applies only within a language game, not to the language game itself or to the practice from which the language arises.

However, Phillips's rejoinder misses the breadth of the fact of relativity. If Wittgenstein's framework is right, then relativity does not apply to it. But the question of whether or not Wittgenstein's framework *is* right is subject to conceptual relativity, and the question of what criteria we must employ to judge whether or not Wittgenstein's framework is right is subject to epistemological relativity. Phillips often writes as if Wittgenstein's insights cannot be questioned. He uses Wittgenstein's account of epistemology as the right account, to oppose Rorty, reformed epistemology, and so on. He holds that it is right that philosophy is descriptive, that certain grammatical insights into the nature of God are right and others wrong, and that grammar is the right criterion (and consensus the wrong one) in determining what should be said of God. Phillips thus makes many claims about what is right and what is not, all of which are subject to the fact of relativity. A noumenon, a thing-in-itself, the unknowable God, and our forms of life may be equally beyond the fact of relativity. Indeed, the logic of the fact of relativity entails that such possibilities cannot definitively be ruled out. However, as soon as we try to give a description of forms of life, make a claim that they are ungrounded, give them one label rather than another, give them any content at all, then the fact of relativity is once more seen to be relevant.

Phillips is misled here, I suggest, by his deep-rooted opposition to the possibility of some alternative perspective, different from our own practices, necessary to be able to consider our practices right or wrong. He argues that we should follow Wittgenstein in denying any such 'transcendent certainty'.[4] But

---

[4] Phillips, *Faith after Foundationalism*, ch. 5.

what of the possibility of God, looking at our practices from a viewpoint external to them? What about one society or individual judging the practices of another? Certainly we must keep some practice to be able to judge any other: but my discussion of fundamental trust is designed to show how we can do this and yet be sceptical about all our practices. Phillips's immanentist bias prevents him from seeing the possibility of judging practices.

This Wittgensteinian bias against transcendence can be seen to rule out the possibility of a God external to our practices: indeed, we have seen the cognitivists raise this very objection. This is an implication which Phillips is keen to counter. He writes that should everyone cease to believe in God, it would not be the end of God, but would be mankind turning its back upon God. This suggests that God is more than, and independent of, our practices.

Yet if this is so, there is a worry of bifurcation in Phillips's position, for he is keen to argue that the notion of a viewpoint external to our practices, from which our practices can be judged, makes no sense. This illustrates the tension involved in Phillips's desire for God to transcend our practices and yet for practices to be our stopping point. Some people have been so overwhelmed by something which appears to them to be beyond practices that practices themselves are viewed in a different light.

Examples of this would include some of the people interviewed by Starbuck and commented upon by William James in his classic work *The Varieties of Religious Experience*. One man tells James of three religious experiences he had and concludes:

In all three instances the certainty that there in outward space there stood *something* was indescribably stronger than the ordinary certainty of companionship when we are in the presence of ordinary living people. The something seemed close to me, and intensely more real than any ordinary perception.[5]

James also refers to a man who told him that 'God is more real to me than any thought or thing or person', and comments that 'probably thousands of unpretending Christians would write an almost identical account'.[6] Perhaps most interestingly, James refers to this account given by a clergyman:

[5] William James, *The Varieties of Religious Experience* (London: Fontana, 1960), 64.  [6] Ibid.

The darkness held a presence that was all the more felt because it was not seen. I could not any more have doubted that *He* was there than that I was. Indeed, I felt myself to be if possible the less real of the two. . . . Since that time no discussion that I have heard of the Proofs of God's existence has been able to shake my faith.[7]

On Phillips's own prescribed philosophical task of pure description, it is clear that these accounts cast doubt upon the correctness of practices previously conceived of as right. Indeed, there is an epistemological change from perceiving reason as the right criterion to judge belief in God's reality to accepting (an 'experience' of) God as the right criterion. Thus, even the practice of giving sense to 'right' and 'wrong' is altered. Practices do seem to be susceptible of truth and falsity—although not all at the same time (the lesson of Neurath's ship)—and any claim about the nature of practices which entails the contrary returns us to the fact of relativity. Hence Phillips's argument that the fact of relativity does not make sense in relation to practices does not hold.

This can perhaps be made more clear by considering part of the argument in Phillips's *Faith after Foundationalism*. In the fifth chapter of the book, Phillips follows Wittgenstein in arguing that epistemic practices are not hypotheses or beliefs about reality. They are simply what we do, and 'there is no necessity, external to our practices, which determines that they are as they are'.[8] There is no conception of how reality is which is external to our practices from which our practices could be judged.

Phillips is not concerned with whether one practice is more correct than another but with the fact (as he sees it) that 'correctness' (and hence relativity) makes no sense when applied to practices. 'It is no good either saying that we simply *trust* that the new or modified epistemic practice is correct or more complete, since our problem is the prior one of giving any sense to the terms "correct" and "complete", whether we speak of knowledge or faith in connection with them.'[9]

Phillips repeatedly presses Wittgenstein's point that opinions, hypotheses, or descriptions are very different from the grammar of language itself. Only the former can be right or wrong, not the latter. While I can agree with the first of these sentences, I find

---

[7] Ibid. 61–2.     [8] Phillips, *Faith after Foundationalism*, 57.     [9] Ibid. 60.

it more difficult to accept the second. Certainly, the grammar of a language is not right or wrong in the way that a hypothesis is right or wrong. However, as Phillips himself admits, there are many uses of right and wrong, and it does not follow from the fact that grammar is not like a hypothesis that it cannot be right or wrong in any sense whatever.

Phillips's further move is to describe practices, such as using a particular grammar, as groundless, and thus neither right nor wrong. Yet this move need not be sanctioned. One practice might be a correct one for a particular individual to adopt, while another might be a wrong one for a particular society. Right and wrong apply to practices in the sense of appropriateness and inappropriateness, or propriety and impropriety; thus the fact of relativity can be seen to apply to practices.

Moreover, Phillips's refusal to allow the possibility of a viewpoint external to practices also falls foul of the fact of relativity. The refusal to allow a God's-eye view, or a wholly objective perspective, any possibility at all, is simply to rely non-relatively upon the practices which we are involved in being the last word. To adopt in this way a personal absolute—the ultimacy of practices —is to adopt a particular fundamental trust—much as Rorty does in the contingency of language or Dilthey in the ultimacy of *Erlebnis*—and thus to be subject to the fact of relativity.

Phillips argues against this that the 'possibility' of a God's-eye view is simply empty, one which has no purchase upon our lives. But it may have purchase upon some people's lives—some traditional Christians, those who believe that there is a paradise to which we will go (and perhaps from which we came) and where such a view might be possible for us, the examples from James, or some great religious figures. To assert what makes sense as possible and what does not (as Phillips does) is once again to come within the fact of relativity, for what might be possible is different for different people.

There is a worry that Phillips is doing what many people have taken Don Cupitt to be doing: namely, collapsing God into talk about God. Phillips seems to limit the proper study of philosophy of religion to language, an immanent phenomenon, rather than a phenomenon which might transcend linguistic practices, such as God. Concentration upon grammar to assess the nature of God—even if it is merely to realize that such assessment is impossible—runs the risk of concentrating so much upon religious language that God (who, Phillips admits, is more than words about him) becomes excluded. Phillips's fundamental trust in the immanent starting-point of language may be below the level of being justified or falsified; but to hold from that fundamental trust that there can be no such thing as a traditionally transcendent God is to adopt a philosophical prejudice which is subject to relativity and which does not square with Phillips's own conception of philosophy as purely descriptive. The relevance of the fact of relativity to Phillips's account of religious language, his concept of God, and his role for philosophy is not diminished by his objections discussed here.

## 2. FUNDAMENTAL TRUST AND RELATIVITY IN SWINBURNE AND PHILLIPS

In this section, I wish to show how Swinburne and Phillips exhibit trust, sometimes seemingly fundamental, in the philosophical and theological frameworks, insights, and criteria related to the cognitive, rationality, and expressibility principles. I want further to argue that the consequence of their fundamental trusts is disparity over the question of the appropriateness of the Proofs.

### (i) *The cognitive principle*

The cognitive principle holds that language about God is factual, and thus capable of verification or falsification. For Swinburne, this is borne out by an empirical survey of what believers take their words to mean; but, for Phillips, we must look at the grammatical use of words about God in their proper context, and this investigation of depth grammar reveals the falsity of the cognitive principle.

In relation to this principle, Swinburne and Phillips both reveal trust in relation to the way in which language (particularly religious language) functions, and the way in which we should assess how language functions. Thus, in my terminology, they exhibit trust in the face of conceptual and epistemological relativity.

In Swinburne's conceptual framework, religious language is

taken to be a method of referring as accurately as possible to the external reality of God. In the Wittgensteinian conceptual framework, reality and language cannot be so easily separated. Language does not refer to reality, but is the medium in which reality is expressed. Here is a situation of disparity over the meaning of religious language; for one tradition, language refers, for the other, language is use.

Similarly, Swinburne and Phillips employ disparate criteria in order to judge what religious language should be taken to mean. Swinburne adopts the empirical criteria of sociological and literary surveys of what believers take their beliefs to mean. Phillips, however, adopts the grammatical criterion of examining the words of religion in their worshipping context. One criterion is empirical, the other grammatical. Although, theoretically, the results of these disparate ways of judging the meaning of religious language could be the same—an empirical and a grammatical account of words about God might come up with an agreed-upon conception, or number of conceptions, of what religious language means—in this practical case no such resolution exists. Swinburne and Phillips differ in what they take religious language to mean, and in what they take believers to mean by religious language. If they shared a common criterion, or sufficiently similar criterion, of judging this, then there would be disagreement, which theoretically could be overcome. However, since they differ and use disparate criteria to reach their conclusions, this element of the debate over the appropriateness of the Proofs cannot be brought to resolution.

### (ii) *The expressibility principle*

The expressibility principle states that God is definable, and that some definitions of God are better than others. For Swinburne, this follows not only from the conception of God found within Christianity, but from the nature of God. If we cannot be fairly sure about God's attributes, then we can have no rational guarantee that we are worshipping the right God. For Phillips, however, defining God is denying his mystery. No definition of God is possible because God is essentially beyond clear and easily formulated presentation. Knowledge of God is to be found in our awareness that we do not know God.

Although Swinburne and Phillips both use the same word 'God', it is clear that their pictures of this concept are largely disparate rather than in disagreement. For Swinburne, God is a definable being, capable of being rationally justified, and belief in God's existence is a factual hypothesis based upon evidence. For Phillips, God is beyond definition and being, beyond hypotheses and facts, beyond evidence and justification. God is at the root of a way of viewing the world, not at its end; God is a practical reality, not a rational existent; God is beyond the limits of human understanding, not within them. Thus Swinburne and Phillips do not share a sufficiently common conception of God to be able to have disagreements about it. Since they have disparate conceptions of God, this element of the debate of the appropriateness of the Proofs cannot be brought into resolution.

The three major kinds of relativity are all relevant to an acceptance or rejection of the expressibility principle. Conceptually, Swinburne and Phillips are dealing with disparate understandings of God, neither of which hold true for the other's framework. Epistemologically, God is definable for Swinburne because we can judge which attributes are appropriate to a perfect being; while for Phillips we cannot judge what God is and is not except by following the grammar of God.

The level of preconceptual relativity is particularly relevant to Phillips here. Phillips argues that there comes a point in philosophy 'where all one can say to one's opponent is, "Well, if you can't see it, that's that!"'.[10] There is a suggestion running through Phillips's writings that in order to understand God (by knowing that one cannot understand him) it is necessary to possess religious insight. The right kind of insight leads to the recognition of true religion. Such insight might overcome conceptual and epistemological relativity, but it is clearly a part of preconceptual relativity. The idea of a proper insight into the nature of God is as subject to relativity as are concepts of God and criteria for judging what God is.

### (iii) *The rationality principle*

The rationality principle holds that philosophy's role is to provide rational justification of the existence of items, either generally

[10] Phillips, *The Concept of Prayer*, 83.

or with particular reference to items the existence of which is contentious. For Swinburne, this philosophical task is one which can quite rightly be applied to the existence of God. Once philosophy has shown the coherence of belief in God, it can move on to the rational justification of that belief. For Phillips, however, philosophy has no business providing rational justifications of beliefs, because justification comes to very different things in different contexts, and because philosophy distorts the nature of what it is studying when it tries to do more than describe. Moreover, in philosophy of religion, belief in God is a groundless belief, one merely held together by religious practices, and this is more fundamental than the notion of philosophical justification.

Once again we are faced with disparity rather than disagreement. Swinburne's conceptual framework views philosophy as a justificatory discipline, while in Phillips's conceptual framework it is descriptive only. Swinburne judges philosophy by its rigour, the cogency of the logic of its arguments, and the power of its ability to be an exemplar of rationality. Phillips's criteria for philosophy, however, are grammatical clarity, conceptual elucidation, and leaving language as it is. Thus Swinburne and Phillips share no common conception of philosophy from which to disagree.

Swinburne's paradigm of philosophy, one of 'clear and rigorous argument',[11] is one widely shared by the philosophical school of which he is a part. From the timbre of their writings, Mackie, Kenny, and Flew would seem to concur with Swinburne's criticism of 'the continental philosophy of Existentialism, which, despite its considerable other merits, has been distinguished by a very loose and sloppy style of argument'.[12] Not only are Swinburne's and Phillips's philosophies disparate, but this is also true of the relation between the Anglo-American empiricist and rationalist type philosophy, and philosophy of a Continental flavour, under which heading one should include Wittgenstein. The disparity is easily illustrated by the Anglo-Continental philosophical situation depicted in Rorty, and by numerous particular examples. Thus Bryan Magee writes for many empiricist philosophers that 'Kierkegaard is only doubtfully a philosopher

---

[11] Swinburne, *The Coherence of Theism*, 7.     [12] Ibid.

in the full sense',[13] and adds that 'I find it difficult to believe that Sartre will survive as a philosopher'.[14] Similarly, Mackie exhibits little understanding of Pascal and Kierkegaard in *The Miracle of Theism*.

Phillips is equally at odds with empiricist philosophy, especially empiricist philosophy of religion, and this is true of other thinkers indebted to Wittgenstein, such as Rhees, Malcolm, and Winch. This school desires to leave everything as it is, not to justify or refute what is before it. Phillips, aware of the divergence between the different schools of philosophy of religion, reveals the need to acknowledge one's own personal preference in such a situation. 'No such agreement exists among philosophers of religion [as exists among philosophers in other spheres]: the nature and purpose of their subject is itself a philosophical controversy. It becomes essential, therefore, to give some indication of what *I* think philosophy can say about religion.'[15] Thus Phillips tacitly illustrates the relativity of an assessment of the proper role of philosophy.

### (iv) *Trust in philosophy of religion*

I wish to illustrate in this section what Swinburne and Phillips seem to have as their objects of fundamental trust, as revealed in their writings. Swinburne uses three principles in his attempt to argue in favour of the existence of God: those of simplicity, credulity, and testimony. I have argued that there are three more deep-seated principles, the cognitive, expressibility, and rationality principles, which are relevant to Swinburne seeing the project of arguing for the existence of God as appropriate. It is these principles, I contend, which are the objects of fundamental trust for Swinburne as a philosopher of religion.

We can see that Swinburne's tacit attitude to these principles fits into what we would expect from trust in them, giving the characterization of trust in Chapter 5. The positive attitude to these principles is inescapable for Swinburne. While the three more superficial principles of simplicity, credulity, and testimony could be given up with some alteration in the argument (the probability

[13] Bryan Magee, *The Great Philosophers* (London: BBC Books, 1987), 116.
[14] Ibid. 276.     [15] Phillips, *The Concept of Prayer*, 1.

of God's existence would then become much closer to a half), the three deeper principles cannot be given up without the entire project of *The Coherence of Theism* and *The Existence of God* becoming mistaken.

Swinburne's attitude to these deeper principles, again tacitly, must be one of uncertainty and therefore of risk. The principles of simplicity, credulity, and testimony are supported by argument; the conclusion that God exists depends upon deft handling of probability calculus; the coherence of the belief that God exists depends upon laid down tests of coherence. However, the appropriateness of given logical arguments in relation to the existence of God, the possibility of finding out by an empirical survey what God actually means, the propriety of defining God: all these cannot be supported by any non-circular argument, for they are the bedrock upon which Swinburne's whole project rests. Their lack of non-circular justification makes an attitude to them one of inescapable uncertainty; hence the holding of these principles involves the risk that one's trust in them might be misplaced.

The trust in these principles results in action and prediction. The action is the very project of trying to justify the existence of God by rational means; the prediction is that such a project can provide useful and appropriate results to the question of the existence of God. Thus the cognitive, expressibility, and rationality principles are objects of fundamental trust for Swinburne.

The fact of relativity means that objects of fundamental trust might themselves be relative. From my discussion, it appears that these three principles are relative to a particular philosophical school and a particular kind of religious belief. To assert that the principles are true *per se*, over and above particular frameworks and sets of criteria, as Swinburne tacitly does, is to go against the logic of the fact of relativity. Equally, however, it goes against the fact of relativity to hold that these principles are not, and could not, be non-relative. All one can do is look at the thinker or school in question, and see what kind of response (if any) he or it has to the fact of relativity. From the discussion in my book, it appears that Swinburne in particular, and the empiricist school of philosophy of religion in general, rarely considers the fact of relativity, and that their tacit responses are not capable of escaping from it.

Phillips's work is mainly a series of *ad hominem* arguments, directed primarily against empiricist and rationalist philosophers, and expositions of what he takes to be Wittgenstein's philosophy of religion. The intention behind his work is not to build up a theory about belief in God, but to bring thinkers away from concentrating on philosophy of religion and back to the primary language of religion. His conception of God, however, is not simply a description of what believers' religious language means, for, as I argued in Chapter 3, no such single meaning of religious language (not even just Christian language) exists. Phillips, for all his desire to return philosophers to primary religious language, exhibits such a positive attitude toward philosophy's role being no more than grammatical description, and toward the ultimacy of practices, that reactions against him have concentrated upon his philosophy rather than his theology.

It is my contention, however, that Phillips's writings reveal a fundamental trust both in the proper role of philosophy and in a particular conception of God. This trust is inescapable in Phillips's writings, because his whole task of grammatical description only makes sense if philosophy is seen in this way (as grammatical description), and because without the conception of God with which he is working, his description would be completely different.

The certainties in Phillips's work are those that flow from trust in a Wittgensteinian philosophical framework and a Wittgensteinian conception of God, and all that this entails. Once these things are taken as true or appropriate, then Phillips can be certain of his conclusions. Nevertheless, to take practices as ultimate, to take God as essentially mysterious, to take philosophy as incapable of more than description; all these are central objects of trust, taken to be true but impossible to support in any non-circular manner. Adopting such objects of trust rests upon the inescapability of uncertainty, and hence involves a risk that one might be wrong.

The trust in this particular conception of philosophy and religion results in action (Phillips's actual project of bringing philosophy back to his preferred brand of religious language and practice) and prediction (that philosophy will prove misguided if it goes beyond description, and that religious language is of one kind rather than another). Thus, the limiting of philosophy to description, the ultimacy of practices, and the Wittgensteinian-inspired understanding of God and of true religion, are objects of fundamental trust for Phillips.

These objects of trust appear relative to Phillips, to the school of philosophy which inspires him, and to some religious movement or group sympathetic to the primacy of God's mysteriousness. To assert that any of these objects of fundamental trust are true *per se* (as Phillips tacitly does) is to fall foul of the logic of the fact of relativity; while similarly to hold that they are not, and could not, be non-relative is to go against the same logic. All that one can do is examine responses of particular thinkers and particular schools to this fact; and in the case of Phillips's reply, which seems typical of the Wittgensteinian school, one can conclude, if my argument is correct, that it does not provide a cogent response to the fact of relativity.

This disparity of fundamental trusts between Swinburne and Phillips, and their respective schools, results in a situation of both surface and depth relativity. The surface relativity is shown in the disparity between what is and is not the case for Swinburne and Phillips: that God is definable or mysterious, that philosophy is justificatory or descriptive, that meaning is reference to reality or use. The depth relativity is shown in the disparity over methods of judgement: by insight, grammar, and primary religious practices for Phillips; by logic, analytical argument, and empirical surveys of believers' accounts of their language for Swinburne.

The disparity which exists between Swinburne and Phillips over the appropriateness of the Proofs need not be taken to imply that all disputes in which this issue is in question will involve disparity. I have suggested the likelihood of this in any conflict between members of the Wittgensteinian school and of the empiricist school. Nevertheless, each particular dispute must be examined on its own merits. There may be disputes about the appropriateness of the Proofs which have sufficient in common in terms of conceptual frameworks, preconceptions, and judgemental criteria to be in disagreement rather than disparate.[16] These disputes would then have to be analysed accordingly. I hope that I have shown in this book, however, that the dispute between Swinburne and Phillips runs more deeply than disagreement.

---

[16] Perhaps between Plantinga and the Dutch reformers.

## 3. THE RELATIVITY OF THE PROOFS

I have argued that an assessment of the appropriateness of the Proofs is relative to a number of philosophically and theologically significant factors: the role of philosophy, the meaning of religious language, one's conception of God, one's criteria for making theological and philosophical judgements, as well as the cultural, historical, psychological and sociological relativity which seemingly affects any assessment of any issue.

However, there is one final factor which plays an important part in the relativity of the appropriateness of the Proofs, a factor which Swinburne and Phillips ignore: namely, the relativity of interpretations of what each Proof is designed to show. In this section I will give a brief indication of how relativity affects interpretations of the Proofs, giving special attention to what I take to be the clearest example of this, namely Anselm's ontological argument.

### (i) *The* a posteriori *proofs*

We have already seen[17] that Swinburne and Phillips provide divergent accounts of how the Proofs should be interpreted. While Swinburne treats them in the standard empiricist way, as arguments designed to give logical support to the conclusion that God exists, he does differ from many historical interpreters by construing them as inductive rather than deductive arguments. Even within contemporary empirical philosophy, there is no agreement over how the Proofs should best be interpreted: Mitchell, for example, prefers to see them as supporting the plausibility rather than the probability of the existence of God, while Plantinga considers 'two dozen or so good theistic arguments',[18] attempting to show that God's existence is as rationally defensible as many other, more widely accepted beliefs.

Phillips, however, finds the Proofs unimpressive as logical arguments. He commends them—and feels that this is what impressed Hume and Kant about them—for the religious insight which lies behind them. Thus, the Cosmological Argument is

---

[17] See Ch. 4, sect. 2(ii).
[18] Alvin Plantinga, 'On Our Knowing God', Lectures 7 and 8.

inspired by the belief that God cannot be talked about in the same way that the world is talked about; while the Teleological Argument pays homage to mankind's awe in the face of the order within nature.

These disparate interpretations of the Proofs illustrate the relativity of trying to give a definitive understanding of *the* Cosmological Argument, *the* Argument from Design, or any of the *a posteriori* Proofs. While not wishing to deny that it is possible to distinguish an example of the Teleological Argument from an example of the Moral Argument, for instance, I do think that there is a relativity of interpretations of how the Proofs are best construed. This can be seen from simply reading characterizations of the Proofs in books on philosophy of religion. Thus, while William Rowe finds the principle of sufficient reason to be the heart of the Cosmological Argument,[19] Richard Swinburne finds it to be the simplicity of God as a final explanation against the complexity of seeing the universe as a brute fact.[20] While Brian Davies sees the Teleological Argument as an argument from design (there is clearly design in the universe and we need to assess if there is sufficient design to support the conclusion that God exists),[21] Anthony Kenny sees it as an argument to design (if design can be shown to be in the universe, then there must needs be a designer).[22] While Kant outlines the Moral Argument as based upon the necessity of the *summum bonum* being done, and the inability of humanity to achieve it,[23] Newman suggests God as the best explanation of our consciences,[24] and Mackie puts forward (and refutes) a moral argument designed to show that values are objective, and that objective values are best explained by reference to the existence of God.[25] Finally, Swinburne construes the argument from religious experience as an attempt to provide evidence for the existence of God being the best explanation of

[19] William Rowe, *Philosophy of Religion: An Introduction* (Encino, Calif.: Dickenson Publishing Co., 1978), ch. 2.        [20] Swinburne, *The Existence of God*, ch. 7.
[21] Brian Davies, *An Introduction to the Philosophy of Religion* (Oxford: Oxford University Press, 1982), ch. 6.
[22] Anthony Kenny, 'The Argument from Design', in Anthony Kenny, *Reason and Religion* (Oxford: Basil Blackwell, 1987).
[23] Immanuel Kant, *Critique of Practical Reason*, trans. L. W. Beck (New York: Liberal Arts Press, 1956), ii, ch. 2.
[24] John Henry Newman, *A Grammar of Assent* (London: Faber and Faber, 1870), ch. 5.        [25] Mackie, *The Miracle of Theism*, 114–18.

this phenomenon,[26] while Schleiermacher[27] and Otto[28] rely upon the feeling of dependence and the experience of the numinous respectively to support a move from religious experience to God.

I have relied primarily upon thinkers within empirical philosophy of religion to construct this list, but the variety of interpretations goes far beyond a particular school of philosophy, as we have seen with the Wittgensteinian interpretation. Perhaps the clearest example of this in the current century has been the existentialist interpretation of the Proofs. Existentialist thinkers have construed the Proofs as attempts to reveal the ultimacy of being rather than as rational justifications of the existence of God.

Thus, Gabriel Marcel sets up the need to think of the Proofs as more than failures of logic:

The fact remains that certain distinguished minds found them adequate, and we cannot simply affirm that we are situated at a more advanced position than they on a road which is the highroad of reason. Don't we have reason instead to assume that something essential is implied in their argument which cannot be completely expressed, something we try to explicate without being altogether confident that we can do so?[29]

Such explications from Marcel and other existentialists have concentrated upon the principle of being. Thus Paul Tillich construes the cosmological and teleological arguments as attempts to show that asking the question of God is inescapable.[30] From man's position of human finitude, he must ask about the infinite, and this is the situation illustrated in the Proofs. The cosmological argument asks the question of being, namely how there can be being at all, while the teleological argument asks the question of meaning, namely how there can be meaning. The necessity of these questions is shown by the analysis of man's anxiety in finitude contained within the Proofs.

[26] Swinburne, *The Existence of God*, ch. 13.

[27] Friedrich Schleiermacher, *On Religion, Addresses to its Cultured Critics*, trans. Terence N. Tice (Richmond, Va.: John Knox Press, 1909).

[28] Rudolf Otto, *The Idea of the Holy*, trans. John W. Harvey (Oxford: Oxford University Press, 1923).

[29] Gabriel Marcel, 'Meditations on the Idea of a Proof for the Existence of God', in Gabriel Marcel, *Creative Fidelity*, trans. Robert Rosthal (New York: Crossroad, 1982), 178.

[30] Paul Tillich, *Systematic Theology*, vol. ii (London: Nisbet and Co., 1953), 227–34.

Karl Jaspers echoes Tillich in using the language of being to interpret the Proofs. They are not intended to demonstrate a being at all, for Jaspers, but the transcendence of the human situation by Being itself:

The *cosmological* argument starts out from the existence of the world, which does not consist of itself. The *teleological* one starts from the purposive design of life and the beauty of mundane things. The *moral* argument starts out from good will, which postulates transcendent being as its own ground and goal. Each time, the rational form and the visual being constitute only the medium in which the experience of discontent brings forth the argument proper. Looking through the veil of the rationalistic language, we see the font of each argument in the existential sense of being it expresses.[31]

This existentialist attitude toward the Proofs shows, even in my brief sketch, how varied interpretations of the Proofs are. These various interpretations suggest that conceptual and epistemological relativity apply even to interpreting what each Proof amounts to. While empiricist philosophers may simply disagree over the logical importance of different varieties of a single argument, their divergence from other schools, such as the Wittgensteinian and the existential, is one of disparity. Their conceptual framework is such that the logical force of the Proofs is primary; but the Wittgensteinian conceptual framework concentrates instead upon the theological import of the Proofs; while existentialism is disparate from each of these with its emphasis upon the transcendence of beings by pointing to Being. The different schools' criteria for assessing how to interpret the Proofs are also disparate: while empiricist philosophy tends to interpret a particular Proof in its logically most cogent form, Wittgensteinians prefer the interpretation with the greatest grammatical insight into religious belief, and existentialists adopt the interpretation which moves away from a God and towards the fact of Being itself.

There is equally relativity in connection with the interpretation of the Proofs by those who find them inappropriate. Thus, while Phillips finds them grammatically inappropriate when construed as logical arguments, Kierkegaard finds them inappropriate

---

[31] Karl Jaspers, *Philosophy*, vol. iii, trans. E. B. Ashton (Chicago and London: University of Chicago Press, 1969), 178.

because belief in the existence of God is in the *improbable* rather than the probable;[32] and Pascal and Bultmann find them inappropriate because human reason adopts an arrogant stance by placing God at its service.[33]

It might be argued that, although there is a relativity of views on how the Proofs are best interpreted, leading to a relativity of answers to the question 'Are the Proofs appropriate when interpreted in their most convincing form?', this is not so for the question if one refers to the Proofs as what they meant to those philosophers who put them forward. However, there are problems here also, for the Proofs have been put forward by many different philosophers, and it is a relative preference which form one takes as historically seminal.

Perhaps, then, we can resort to the situation in which relativity seems least involved, and ask, 'Is the cosmological argument appropriate as it was put forward by Leibniz?', or, 'Is the teleological argument appropriate, as put forward by Paley?', and so on. One could then concentrate upon a particular text, thus providing a focus for interpretation. Rather than asking, 'Is *the* particular proof appropriate?', we can discuss the appropriateness of one thinker's interpretation of a proof. Although this cannot avoid all the areas where relativity has been found to be relevant, discussed throughout the latter half of this book, surely here is one area in which the fact of relativity cannot apply.

I wish to suggest that this is not so. Although there is probably more agreement over the meaning of the *a posteriori* Proofs in philosophers' writings than over the ontological argument, there are still divergences of interpretation: witness the various interpretations which have been given of Kant's philosophy, for example, which can only result in divergent interpretations of how he understood the Moral Argument. Although the relativity of interpretations of what the *a posteriori* Proofs meant to those who put them forward has limited application, then, it is more clearly

---

[32] Kierkegaard, *Philosophical Fragments*, 94 n.: 'Generally speaking, the idea . . . of seriously wanting to link a probability proof to the improbable . . . is so stupid that one could deem its occurrence impossible.'

[33] Pascal, *Pensées*, no. 190, p. 86. Rudolf Bultmann, *Faith and Understanding*: 'To speak of God in this sense [to argue about his existence] is not only error and without meaning—it is sin.' (*Faith and Understanding*, vol. i, trans. Lewis Pettibone Smith (London: SCM Press, 1969), 54.)

seen in the context of Anselm's argument in *Proslogion* II–IV, and it is to this which I now turn.

### (ii) *The ontological argument*

I am not aware of a finer treatment of the variety of the interpretations of a particular philosophical argument than Arthur McGill's paper on Anselm's ontological proof.[34] Anselm's argument, after being ignored or scornfully dismissed for centuries, has certainly engendered a widespread reaction in modern times. The issues involved in interpreting Anselm's argument are many, and all result in divergent opinions: whether *Proslogion* II (the traditional interpretation) or *Proslogion* III (the modern interpretation) is the heart of the argument; if *Proslogion* III is the centre, then whether the first part of the chapter (Barth) or the second part (Stolz) is more important; whether the argument cannot stand up to Kant's famous criticism that existence is not a predicate (still widely held today, by Swinburne, for example) or whether *Proslogion* III overcomes the objection by moving from God's existence to his necessary existence (Malcolm, Hartshorne); and whether the argument is meant to be a proof (the traditional interpretation), a piece of grammatical insight (Malcolm, Phillips), or a religious tract intended primarily as prayer (Barth).

In this section, I will concentrate upon one particular example to show that, even given a single, brief text, a relativity of interpretations can result. This example is how one should interpret the 'idea' of God which the Fool has. McGill, in dismissing the suggestion that this idea is purely a human idea (for it is impossible to prove the real existence of the object of any human idea), gives a lucid summary of the interpretations of the idea of God given over the history of philosophy.

Very briefly, these are sixfold. First, the idea is a realistic idea; in other words, a direct awareness of reality. The objections here are that Anselm often argues against the possibility of direct awareness of God, and this interpretation assumes another controversial thesis, that Anselm is working entirely within a Platonic framework. Secondly, the idea is a noetic datum; in other words,

---

[34] Arthur McGill, 'Recent Discussions of Anselm's Argument', in John Hick and Arthur McGill (eds.), *The Many-Faced Argument* (New York: Macmillan, 1967). All page-references in this section are to this work.

God is the cause of our idea of him. The worry here is that we seem to be reading Descartes's argument back into Anselm. Thirdly, the idea is a noetic limit; we all come up against the boundary concept of that than which nothing greater can be conceived. The problems here are that we seem to be reading existentialism back into Anselm; and it is a dubious psychological assertion that we all come up against such a noetic limit. Fourthly, the idea of God is seen as reflexive; the idea is at the root of all our thinking, perceived when we look within rather than without. This interpretation seems mistaken because it ascribes to Anselm the equating of the highest in man with God, whereas Anselm consistently keeps a deep gulf between God and created reality. Fifthly, the idea comes from revelation. This reading of Anselm is particularly questionable, because Anselm disavows any proof from authority, and the role of the Fool becomes very hard to explain. Finally, the idea is one proved in the *Monologion*; Anselm himself disavows any such interpretation with his stated intent that the *Proslogion* is meant to stand entirely on its own.

Rather than despairing of giving a definitive interpretation of Anselm's argument, McGill provides his own suggestion. His interest is in the fact that the fool *says* in his heart that there is no God. He draws attention to the fact that Chapter 2 begins with the fool saying that God is not, and understanding the phrase 'something than which nothing greater can be conceived' when he hears it spoken. Moreover, Anselm argues that the fool is convinced that 'something than which nothing greater can be conceived' stands in relation to his understanding because he understands it when he hears it.

When Gaunilo questions this, Anselm affirms that 'in my argument nothing else is needed except uttering the words, "that than which a greater cannot be conceived"'.[35] McGill concludes from this that Anselm is 'convinced that hearing words is an event of genuine knowledge; that words themselves have the power to initiate some kind of relation of "understanding" between the listening mind and reality' (p. 106). Anselm is aware that the word 'God' is not readily understandable; and this is why he uses a formula instead that is comprised of readily

[35] Anselm, *Reply*, V (I. 135. 19 f.), trans. Arthur McGill.

comprehensible words. The fool can understand these words because of this, and can therefore conceive of God. He thus becomes cognizant of the meaning of the word God; and although one could conceive of any other term and not thereby know whether or not it existed, it is part of the uniqueness of Anselm's formula that once one conceives of it, its existence cannot logically be denied.

McGill argues that interpretations of Anselm have missed this point because of the theory of language inherited from the seventeenth century. While for Anselm, and for centuries afterwards, there was a distinction between knowledge through words and knowledge through experience, this distinction was destroyed by the seventeenth-century conviction that all knowledge comes through experience. We can now see this error because of theories of language such as Heidegger's, and this will enable us to reassess the Anselmian ontological argument properly. For McGill, 'Anselm rests his argument on the power of verbal statements to convey their objective meaning' (p. 108).

Since McGill's essay, more interest has been shown in Anselm's theory of language. G. R. Evans, for example, has emphasized the difference between *voces* and *naturalia verba*. Gaunilo correctly objects against Anselm that we cannot infer the existence of the perfect island from *voces* about it. Anselm can agree because he does not speak of *voces* at all; rather he holds that God is a special case, and that although we can deny that God exists in ordinary words, we cannot do so in *naturalia verba*.

The understanding engendered by *naturalia verba* lies at the limit of our ordinary language and understanding for Evans. The Wittgensteinian interest is obvious when he writes that 'the fact that we cannot think of God because he lies at the limit of our understanding, except as the very thought which does lie at the limit of our understanding, is exactly what Anselm wants his readers to accept'.[36] We can deny the existence of God in ordinary words, those which we use away from the limit of our understanding; but in *naturalia verba*, which we use at that limit, there can be no such denial.

Perhaps the best example of a recent account of Anselm

---

[36] G. R. Evans, *Anselm and Talking about God* (Oxford: Clarendon Press, 1978), 74.

influenced by McGill's proposal is Richard Campbell's. He argues that the starting-point of chapter 2 is Anselm's saying 'something than which nothing greater can be thought'. Using Austin's term, Campbell calls this a speech act rather than a premiss. He continues that Anselm's theory of language was much like Wittgenstein's; in other words, that language is a public and not a private matter. Anselm's speech act is perfectly intelligible because the formula uses terms that are publicly comprehensible. For Campbell,

his point is that, since these words [of the formula] are significant, and can be understood, there can be no question but that something so described can be thought of. The relation between words and thought is not just accidental; thought is always specifiable in terms of words.[37]

It is fascinating to note that on Campbell's interpretation Anselm's argument is *a posteriori* and not *a priori* at all because it begins with the empirical event of the fool hearing Anselm speak of 'something than which nothing greater can be conceived'. The argument does not rest upon an impersonal premiss, but a speech act. Similarly, the conclusion is not impersonal; rather, it is the resolution of the personal conflict between the believer and the fool, who are using a common language but are reaching different conclusions about the existence of that which is described in the common language.

For Campbell, 'the understanding Anselm achieves is one available to the fool as well, if only he will think through what is involved in his understanding of the piece of public language used by the believer to state his belief'.[38] If one follows Anselm's argument through, then the conclusion must be that the way in which the fool uses Anselm's formula is incoherent. The fool is denying that which cannot be denied. Against Malcolm, 'it is a consequence of the Argument that atheism is not an intelligible position'.[39]

However, this is only a consequence from the religious language which Anselm chooses to use. Such a choice is not arbitrary; it is governed by Anselm's own religious life. Anselm's enquiry is designed primarily to lead him to understand his belief. This

---

[37] Richard Campbell, *From Belief To Understanding* (Canberra: The Australian National University, 1976), 44.
[38] Ibid. 197.        [39] Ibid. 201.

explains his initial reaction to Gaunilo's objection: 'Since the fool against whom I spoke in my little work does not refute me in these statements, but someone not a fool, who is a Catholic speaking on behalf of the fool, it is enough for me to reply to the Catholic.'[40] Anselm's argument is not idle speculation, but is rooted in the religious context. Thus the words of the formula are part of the language of faith, suggesting an interpretation such as Barth's; but equally they are part of public language, thus ruling Barth's interpretation out of court. The purely rational or purely faithful dichotomy that is usually offered to Anselm is ruled out by Campbell: 'The genius of Anselm's theological method consists in the way he is at once *engagé*, committed to the God he is addressing, and at the same time rational, developing arguments and drawing conclusions.'[41]

The problem with Anselm's ontological argument for Campbell is that we do not live in a society in which it is widely accepted that God is the most exalted being, above all else. This makes the argument plausible only for that limited number of Christians who accept Anselm's initial description. Thus it is not as easy in current society as it was in Anselm's to envisage 'something than which nothing greater can be conceived'.

Unsurprisingly, this kind of interpretation of Anselm has called forth criticism. One notable critic has been Robert Brecher, who accuses Campbell of 'too much Wittgensteinian hindsight'.[42] For Brecher, the role of the fool has been underestimated by Campbell, who, as we have seen, emphasizes the addressing of Gaunilo specifically as a Catholic and Anselm as concerned to understand his own belief. Brecher, on the other hand, argues that the formula is an agreed definition exemplifying the shared metaphysics of Anselm and the fool: that reality admits of degrees. Although Campbell is aware of this, he does not take it fully into account, according to Brecher.

For Brecher, the point of Anselm's reference to Gaunilo being a Catholic is that to refute Gaunilo one can presume shared religious assumptions; whereas in the case of the fool no such assumptions exist. This is why Anselm gives his formula which

[40] Anselm, *Reply*, Introduction (I. 130. 3–5).
[41] Campbell, *From Belief To Understanding*, 203.
[42] Robert Brecher, *Anselm's Argument* (Aldershot: Gower, 1985), 4.

assumes degrees of reality, for it is a metaphysical system that he and the fool share. Anselm's argument becomes the existence of God inferred from a shared metaphysics. Thus the argument is not at all dependent upon the religious context; it is an unavowedly philosophical argument.

I think that Brecher's reply reveals something ineradicable about Anselm scholarship. His objection is essentially that his interpretation is a better one than Campbell's; and therefore Campbell's is wrong. Hidden behind this is the assumption that there is a paradigm interpretation of Anselm's argument. It is this assumption that I wish to contest. There is simply insufficient evidence to decide whether Brecher's or Campbell's interpretation is the better one. Brecher is noticeably reticent over the fact that Anselm says his formula and that the fool hears it; nor does he have much to say about the religious context of the argument. Equally he is right that Campbell gives little attention to the metaphysical background of the formula. What we have is two interpreters stressing different aspects of the Anselmian argument. I suggest that this appears to be unavoidable—human beings are bound to have different emphases reflecting their own unique reading of a text and their own interests—and that consequently there appears to be no one definitive interpretation of Anselm.

The fact of relativity applies even to interpreting the written texts from which we take the Proofs; implying that a definitive interpretation of even a particular thinker's version of a Proof is unlikely, but not entailing that such an interpretation is impossible, for this too falls foul of the logic of the fact of relativity.

It is interesting that Campbell seems to concur with this. The concluding sentences of his book are:

A confrontation with a thinker of Anselm's penetration and insight can lead to the exposing of our own intellectual inadequacies. But since this process of dialogue is living and dramatic in character, neither I nor anyone else can fairly claim to have said the last word.[43]

McGill has similar reservations. Throughout his reinterpretation of Anselm as presuming a Heidegger-type theory of language, we encounter phrases such as 'he is convinced, apparently', 'he seems to be groping toward', and 'it might be argued that'.

---

[43] Campbell, *From Belief To Understanding*, 227.

Sometimes he seems to be firmer in his account than at others; but there is clearly a residual doubt in his own mind about his interpretation of Anselm.

Furthermore, McGill bases much of his interpretation upon other writings by Anselm, whereas Anselm himself tells us that the *Proslogion* is supposed to stand as a single piece of reasoning. One suspects that other writings of Anselm could be used equally well to support other accounts of his intentions; certainly McGill's argument has not been taken as textually unimpeachable. It appears that, rather than putting an end to the typology of interpretations of Anselm as McGill wished to do, he and Campbell and others have produced a new kind of interpretation to add to the list.

McGill himself feels that if no definitive interpretation of Anselm's argument is possible, then the worry is that any interpretation is acceptable:

Considering the labor that has been expended and yet the continuing failure of every interpretation to escape points of awkwardness, we might conclude that the project is impossible, that sufficient data do not exist—either in Anselm's own corpus or in the extant remnants from his age—to settle our questions about his argument. Apparently any commentator can look at the text from his own perspective and can find just enough evidence there to warrant his own particular theory. (p. 104)

I suggest that McGill is going too far here. The existence of the text means that some interpretations can be ruled out as simply impossible. Anselm's argument is not a piece of liberation theology, or process theology,[44] for example. The worry that if there is no definitive interpretation then any interpretation is possible rests upon presenting a false dichotomy between a definitive interpretation and any interpretation. There is a third option which McGill does not consider; namely, the possibility of several, equally textually accurate, interpretations which, although reflecting the commentator's own philosophical and theological interests, are constrained in what they say by the text itself.

---

[44] Indeed, the process theologian Hartshorne argues that this is the weakness of Anselm's argument. See *The Logic of Perfection* (La Salle, Ill.: Open Court, 1962), 33: 'If perfection or divinity must be defined and conceived as Anselm, Descartes, and many another philosopher or theologian, conceived it, then I hold that the Proof amounts to a cogent argument against theism.'

This third option allows for the relating of twentieth-century interests to an argument of such subtlety and insight that its eleventh-century concerns are not dissimilar from them. Barth's theology, Tillich's and Jaspers's existentialism, McGill's Heidegger-influenced interest in the noetic power of words, Campbell's and Malcolm's Wittgenstein-influenced interest in the grammatical structure of religious belief: all these reflect the relativity of modern philosophical and theological concerns, and yet we are prevented from an anarchy of interpretations of Anselm's argument by the text itself.

Thus we have one further element which entails the relevance of the fact of relativity to the appropriateness of the Proofs. Even attempting to interpret the original meaning of an actual argument, and particularly Anselm's ontological argument, does not result in a single definitive account. The history of the variety of interpretations of Anselm's argument is not ended by McGill's suggestion, nor need this result in the acceptability of any interpretation of the argument. Rather, we see the relevance of the fact of relativity to interpreting the meaning and intent of the Proofs. The interpretations of the Proofs we have considered have all been shown to be relative to the particular interpreter's philosophical and theological concerns; and yet to hold that all such interpretations are always no more than relative is to go against the fact of relativity. All that one can conclude is that, given the interpretations of Anselm's argument of which we are aware, none seems to go beyond the fact of relativity.

## 4. CONCLUSION

I have argued in this book that the issue of the appropriateness of the Proofs of the existence of God is treated in an unsatisfactory manner by Swinburne and Phillips, and also by the philosophical schools of which they are a part, in so far as they ignore, or fail to see the full significance of, the fact of relativity, and the consequent need for a notion such as fundamental trust.

For Swinburne and those of his philosophical bent, which includes the mainstream of Anglo-American philosophy of religion, there is a fundamental trust in the cognitive, expressibility, and rationality principles. It is this trust which I have tried to bring out in this book, as lying behind the comparatively superficial characteristics of this school usually discussed in the literature (such as logical validity, balance of probabilities, and coherence). For Phillips and the Wittgensteinian school generally, the fundamental trust lies in the limiting of philosophy to grammatical description, the impossibility of going beyond practices, and the consequences of this for the meaning of religious language and particularly the concept of God.

It has not been my intention to attempt to adjudicate between these two sets of fundamental trust. Indeed, my argument has been that no such adjudication is possible, because the fundamental trusts and their objections stand in a situation of disparity rather than disagreement. Rather, I have tried to show how the fact of relativity leads to such disparity.

I have done this by distinguishing several kinds of relativity, relevant to the appropriateness of the Proofs. Conceptual relativity is present particularly in the different concepts of God, philosophy, and language, and in the different overall conceptual frameworks, possessed by the two philosophical schools. Preconceptual relativity is present particularly in the Wittgen-steinian idea of religious or grammatical insight allowing us to look and see how things are. Epistemological relativity is present in the disparate criteria which the two philosophical schools use to judge the appropriateness of the Proofs: a sociological and literary survey of what believers have taken their religious language to mean on the one side, and a grammatical description of religious language in its primary religious context on the other. Finally, in the previous section I have argued that there is also a relativity of interpretation, a reflection of one's own, or one's school's, philosophical interests which impinges upon how one construes the Proofs. Thus Swinburne finds the Proofs appropriate as logical arguments, while Phillips finds them inappropriate viewed in this light but appropriate when construed as pieces of grammatical insight designed to give glory to God.

I have repeatedly given the caveat that one's attitude to the fact of relativity is itself uncertain. To assert the non-relativity of this fact is to assert an absolute against its own logic; but equally to hold that the fact is itself relative is to deny in a non-relative manner the possibility of absolutes. This uncertainty in the face of relativity provides cogent support for my suggestion that it is an attitude such as trust, which occurs in the face of the uncertain, that underlies one's response to the question of the appropriateness of the Proofs.

It might be argued that, faced with the relativity of the appropriateness of the Proofs, study of the Proofs should be given up, for they do not provide a neutral example of philosophical argument at work, or cogent support for the existence of God. We have seen a similar worry in McGill's paper, that if no definitive interpretation of Anselm's argument is possible, the study of it becomes futile because any interpretation will do.

I suggested, in the face of McGill's worry, that the need for differing interpretations of Anselm is actually positive, because it reflects the breadth of Anselm's philosophical and theological concerns and their relevance to those of modern thinkers. The same is true of the issue of the appropriateness of the Proofs. The relevance of the issue to central philosophical and theological topics, such as the meaning of language, the proper role of philosophy, the nature of God, relativity, philosophical disagreement and disparity, and the existential importance of trust, implies the worth of the Proofs. The fact of relativity suggests that the kind of debate indulged in many centuries ago by Clement and Tertullian may always be with us: and the profound and central issues raised by any serious debate over the appropriateness of the Proofs of God's existence suggests that this is a situation which we should welcome.

# BIBLIOGRAPHY

The date of the original publication of each work is given in parentheses at the end of the entry.

ANSELM, ST, *Proslogion and Reply to Gaunilo*, trans. M. J. Charlesworth (Oxford: Clarendon Press, 1965). (1077–8)

AQUINAS, ST THOMAS, *Summa Theologiae*, II, Ia, 2–11, trans. Timothy McDermott (Oxford: Blackfriars, 1963). (1265–8)

BARTH, KARL, *Anselm: Fides quarens intellectum*, trans. Ian W. Robertson (London: SCM Press, 1960).

—— *Church Dogmatics*, vol. i, pt. 1, trans. G. T. Thomson, 2nd edn. (Edinburgh: T. and T. Clark, 1969). (1936)

BERGER, PETER, *A Rumour of Angels* (London: Allen Lane, 1969).

BERNSTEIN, RICHARD, *Beyond Objectivism and Relativism* (Oxford: Basil Blackwell, 1983).

BEZANTOS, ROMAN J., 'Wilhelm Dilthey: An Introduction', in Wilhelm Dilthey, *Introduction to the Human Sciences*, trans. Roman J. Bezantos (London: Harvester, 1988). (1923)

BOWKER, JOHN, *The Sense of God* (Oxford: Clarendon Press, 1973).

BRECHER, ROBERT, *Anselm's Argument* (Aldershot: Gower, 1985).

BRUNNER, EMIL, and BARTH, KARL, *Natural Theology*, trans. Peter Fraenkel (London: SCM Press, 1943). (1934)

BULTMANN, RUDOLF, *Faith and Understanding*, vol. i, trans. Lewis Pettibone Smith (London: SCM Press, 1969). (1933)

—— 'Is Exegesis Without Presuppositions Possible?', trans. Schubert M. Ogden, in *Existence and Faith: Shorter Writings of Rudolf Bultmann* (London: Fontana, 1964), 342–51. (1957)

CAMPBELL, RICHARD, *From Belief to Understanding* (Canberra: The Australian National University, 1976).

CRAIG, WILLIAM LANE, *The Cosmological Argument from Plato to Leibniz* (London: Macmillan, 1980).

CUPITT, DON, *Taking Leave of God* (London: SCM Press, 1980).

DAVIES, BRIAN, *An Introduction to the Philosophy of Religion* (Oxford: Oxford University Press, 1982).

DILTHEY, WILHELM, *Der Junge Dilthey: Letters and Diary 1852–1870*, selected by Clara Misch-Dilthey (Leipzig and Berlin, 1933).

—— *The Essence of Philosophy*, trans. Stephen A. and William T. Emery (Chapel Hill, NC: University of North Carolina Press, 1954). (1924)

ERMATH, MICHAEL, *Wilhelm Dilthey: The Critique of Historical Reason* (Chicago: University of Chicago Press, 1978).

EVANS, G. R., *Anselm and Talking about God* (Oxford: Clarendon Press, 1978).

FLEW, ANTONY, *God and Philosophy* (London: Hutchinson, 1966).

—— et al., 'Theology and Falsification', in Antony Flew and Alasdair Macintyre (eds.), *New Essays in Philosophical Theology* (London: SCM Press, 1955).

GAMBETTA, DIEGO (ed.), *Trust: Making and Breaking Co-operative Relations* (Oxford: Basil Blackwell, 1988).

GASKIN, J. C. A., *Hume's Philosophy of Religion* (London: Macmillan, 1978).

GOULDER, MICHAEL, and HICK, JOHN, *Why Believe in God?* (London: SCM Press, 1983).

HARTSHORNE, CHARLES, *The Logic of Perfection* (La Salle, Ill.: Open Court, 1962).

—— *Anselm's Discovery* (La Salle, Ill.: Open Court, 1965).

HENRY, DESMOND PAUL, *The Logic of Saint Anselm* (Oxford: Clarendon Press, 1967).

HICK, JOHN, 'Theology and Verification', *Theology Today*, xvii (1 Apr. 1960).

—— 'Sceptics and Believers', in John Hick (ed.), *Faith and the Philosophers* (London: Macmillan, 1964).

—— 'The Justification of Religious Belief', *Theology*, lxxxi (Mar. 1968), 100–7.

—— *Arguments for the Existence of God* (New York: Herder, 1971).

—— *Faith and Knowledge*, 2nd edn. (London: Macmillan, 1973). (1957)

—— *God and the Universe of Faiths* (London: Macmillan Press, 1973).

—— *Evil and the God of Love*, 2nd edn. (London: Macmillan, 1977). (1966)

—— 'Remarks', in Stuart C. Brown (ed.), *Reason and Religion* (London: Cornell University Press, 1977), 122–8.

—— *Philosophy of Religion*, 3rd edn. (Englewood Cliffs, NJ: Prentice Hall, 1983). (1963)

—— 'Religious Realism and Non-Realism: Defining the Issue', unpublished paper given at Philosophy of Religion Conference at Claremont Graduate School, Claremont, Calif., and later at the University of Birmingham, 1988.

—— *An Interpretation of Religion* (Basingstoke: Macmillan, 1989).

—— (ed.), *The Existence of God* (New York: Macmillan Press, 1964).

—— and MCGILL, ARTHUR (eds.), *The Many-Faced Argument* (New York: Macmillan, 1967).

HODGES, H. A., *Wilhelm Dilthey: An Introduction* (London: Kegan Paul, Trench, Trubner and Co., 1944).

—— *The Philosophy of Wilhelm Dilthey* (London: Routledge and Kegan Paul, 1952).

HOLLIS, MARTIN, and LUKES, STEVEN (eds.), *Rationality and Relativism* (Oxford: Basil Blackwell, 1982).

HUDSON, W., *Wittgenstein and Religious Belief* (London: Macmillan, 1975).

HUME, DAVID, *Dialogues Concerning Natural Religion* (Oxford: Clarendon Press, 1935). (1776)

JAMES, E. O., *The Concept of Deity* (London: Hutchinson's University Library, 1950).

JAMES, WILLIAM, *The Varieties of Religious Experience* (London: Fontana, 1960). (1901–2)

JASPERS, KARL, *Philosophy*, vol. iii, trans. E. B. Ashton (Chicago and London: University of Chicago Press, 1969). (1932)

JASPERT, BERND (ed.), *Karl Barth—Rudolf Bultmann: Letters 1922–1966*, trans. Geoffrey W. Bromley (Edinburgh: T. and T. Clark, 1982).

KANT, IMMANUEL, *Critique of Practical Reason*, trans. L. W. Beck (New York: Liberal Arts Press, 1956), ii, ch. 22. (1788)

KAUFMAN, GORDON, *Relativism, Knowledge and Faith* (Chicago: University of Chicago Press, 1960).

—— *Systematic Theology* (New York: Charles Scribner's Sons, 1968).

—— *God: The Problem* (Cambridge, Mass.: Harvard University Press, 1972).

—— *An Essay on Theological Method* (Missoula, Mont.: Scholars Press, 1975).

—— *The Theological Imagination* (Philadelphia: The Westminster Press, 1981).

KEIGHTLEY, ALAN, *Wittgenstein, Grammar and God* (London: Epworth Press, 1976).

KENNY, ANTHONY, *The Five Ways* (London: Routledge and Kegan Paul, 1969).

—— 'In Defence of God', *Times Literary Supplement* (7 Feb. 1975), 145.

—— *The God of the Philosophers* (Oxford: Clarendon Press, 1979).

—— *Faith and Reason* (New York: Columbia University Press, 1983).

—— *A Path from Rome* (London: Sidgwick and Jackson, 1985).

—— 'The Argument from Design', in Anthony Kenny, *Reason and Religion* (Oxford: Basil Blackwell, 1987), 69–84. (1986)

KERR, FERGUS, *Theology after Wittgenstein* (Oxford: Basil Blackwell, 1986).

KIERKEGAARD, SØREN, *Concluding Unscientific Postscript*, trans. D. F. Swenson (Princeton, NJ: Princeton University Press, 1941). (1846)

—— *Philosophical Fragments*, trans. D. F. Swenson (Princeton, NJ: Princeton University Press, 1985).

KOLAKOWSKI, LESZEK, *Religion* (Oxford: Oxford University Press, 1982).

—— 'The Worshippers' God and the Philosophers' God', *Times Literary Supplement* (23 May 1986), 567–8.

KUNG, HANS, *Does God Exist?*, trans. Edward Quinn (London: Collins, 1980).

LOCKE, JOHN, *An Essay Concerning Human Understanding* (Oxford: Clarendon Press, 1975). (1689)

LUHMANN, NIKLAS, *Trust and Power*, trans. Howard Davies *et al.* (Chichester: John Wiley and Sons, 1979).

MACINTYRE, ALASDAIR, 'Relativism, Power and Philosophy', in *Proceedings and Addresses of the American Philosophical Association*, 1985, pp. 5–22.

MACKIE, JOHN, *The Miracle of Theism* (Oxford: Clarendon Press, 1982).

MACQUARRIE, JOHN, *Twentieth Century Religious Thought* (London: SCM Press, 1981).

—— *In Search of Deity* (London: SCM Press, 1984).

MAGEE, BRYAN, *The Great Philosophers* (London: BBC Books, 1987).

MAKKREEL, RUDOLF, *Dilthey: Philosopher of the Human Studies* (Princeton, NJ: Princeton University Press, 1975).

MALCOLM, NORMAN, *Ludwig Wittgenstein: A Memoir* (London: Oxford University Press, 1958).

—— *Knowledge and Certainty* (Englewood Cliffs, NJ: Prentice Hall, 1963).

—— 'Is it a Religious Belief that God Exists?', in John Hick (ed.), *Faith and the Philosophers* (London: Macmillan, 1964).

—— 'The Groundlessness of Belief', in Stuart C. Brown (ed.), *Reason and Religion* (London: Cornell University Press, 1977), 143–85.

—— *Nothing is Hidden* (Oxford: Basil Blackwell, 1986).

MARCEL, GABRIEL, 'Meditations on the Idea of a Proof for the Existence of a God', in Gabriel Marcel, *Creative Fidelity*, trans. Robert Rosthal (New York: Crossroad, 1982), 175–83. (1964)

MARGOLIS, JOSEPH, *Pragmatism without Foundations* (New York and Oxford: Basil Blackwell, 1986).

MARSH, ROBERT CHARLES, 'The Function of Criticism in Philosophy', *Proceedings of the Aristotelian Society*, 53 (1953), 135–50.

MARTIN, DEAN, '*On Certainty* and Religious Belief', *Religious Studies* 20 (1984), 593–613.

MEILAND, JACK W., and KRAUSZ, MICHAEL (eds.), *Relativism: Cognitive and Moral* (Notre Dame, Ind.: University of Notre Dame Press, 1982).

MITCHELL, BASIL, *The Justification of Religious Belief* (London: Macmillan, 1973).

MOORE, GARETH, 'Review of *Faith after Foundationalism*', *New Blackfriars*, 71 (Mar. 1990), 151–4.

MORAWETZ, THOMAS, *Wittgenstein and Knowledge* (Amherst, Mass.: University of Massachusetts Press, 1978).

MUELLER-VOLLMER, K., *Towards a Phenomenological Theory of Literature* (The Hague: Mouton and Co., 1963).

NEWMAN, JOHN HENRY, *A Grammar of Assent* (London: Faber and Faber, 1870).

NIEBUHR, H. RICHARD, *Radical Monotheism and Western Culture* (London: Faber and Faber, 1943).

—— *Christ and Culture* (New York: Harper and Row, 1951).

NIETZSCHE, FRIEDRICH, *Beyond Good and Evil*, trans. Helen Zimmern (Edinburgh and London: T. N. Foulis, 1909).

NISHITANI, KEIJI, *Religion and Nothingness*, trans. Jan Van Brogt (Berkeley, Calif.: University of California Press, 1982).

OTTO, RUDOLF, *The Idea of the Holy*, trans. John W. Harvey (Oxford: Oxford University Press, 1923). (1917)

OWEN, H. P., *Concepts of Deity* (London and Basingstoke: Macmillan, 1971).

PANNENBERG, WOLFHART, *What is Man?*, trans. Duane A. Priebe (Philadelphia: Fortress Press, 1970).

PASCAL, BLAISE, *Pensées*, trans. A. Krailsheimer (Harmondsworth: Penguin, 1985). (1659)

PHILLIPS, D. Z., *The Concept of Prayer* (New York: Schocken Books, 1966).

—— 'Introduction' to D. Z. Phillips (ed.), *Religion and Understanding* (Oxford: Basil Blackwell, 1968), 1–7.

—— *Death and Immortality* (London and Basingstoke: Macmillan, 1970).

—— *Faith and Philosophical Enquiry* (London: Routledge and Kegan Paul, 1970).

—— *Religion without Explanation* (Oxford: Basil Blackwell, 1976).

—— *Through a Darkening Glass: Philosophy, Literature and Cultural Change* (Oxford: Basil Blackwell, 1982).

—— 'The Devil's Disguises: Philosophy of Religion, "Objectivity" and "Cultural Divergence"', in Stuart C. Brown (ed.), *Objectivity and Cultural Divergence* (Cambridge: Cambridge University Press, 1984), 61–77.

—— 'The Friends of Cleanthes', *Modern Theology*, i/2 (Jan. 1985), 91–104.

—— *Belief, Change and Forms of Life* (Basingstoke: Macmillan, 1986).

—— 'On Not Understanding God', unpublished paper delivered at the University of Birmingham, Oct. 1987.

—— *Faith after Foundationalism* (London: Routledge, 1988).

PIEPER, JOSEF, *The Silence of St Thomas*, trans. Daniel O'Connor (London: Faber and Faber, 1957).

PLANTINGA, ALVIN, 'The Reformed Objection to Natural Theology', in *Proceedings of the American Catholic Association*, 1980, pp. 49–62.

—— 'Is Belief in God Properly Basic?', *Nous*, 15 (1981), 41–51.

—— 'Rationality and Religious Belief', in Steven M. Cahn and David Schatz (eds.), *Contemporary Philosophy of Religion* (New York and Oxford: Oxford University Press, 1982), 255–77.

—— 'Reason and Belief in God', in Alvin Plantinga and Nicholas Wolterstorff (eds.), *Faith and Rationality* (Notre Dame, Ind.: University of Notre Dame Press, 1983), 16–93.

PLANTINGA, ALVIN, 'On Our Knowing God', the unpublished Wilde Lectures given at Oxford University, Trinity Term, 1988.

PLANTINGA, THEODORE, *Historical Understanding in the Thought of Wilhelm Dilthey* (Toronto: University of Toronto Press, 1980).

POJMAN, LOUIS J., *The Logic of Subjectivity* (Tuscaloosa, Ala.: University of Alabama Press, 1984).

POLANYI, MICHAEL, *Science, Faith and Society* (London: Oxford University Press, 1946).

—— *The Study of Man* (London: Routledge and Kegan Paul, 1958).

—— 'The Unaccountable Element in Science', *Philosophy*, 37 (1962), 1–14.

RESCHER, NICHOLAS, 'Philosophical Disagreement', *Review of Metaphysics*, 32 (1978), 217–51.

RHEES, RUSH, *Without Answers* (London: Routledge and Kegan Paul, 1969).

—— *Discussions of Wittgenstein* (London: Routledge and Kegan Paul, 1970).

—— 'Wittgenstein on Language and Ritual', in Brian McGuiness (ed.), *Wittgenstein and his Times* (Oxford: Basil Blackwell, 1982), 69–107.

—— (ed.) *Recollections of Wittgenstein* (Oxford: Oxford University Press, 1984).

RICKMAN, H. P., *Wilhelm Dilthey, Pioneer of the Human Studies* (London: Paul Elek, 1979).

—— *Dilthey Today: A Critical Appraisal of the Contemporary Relevance of his Work* (Westport, Conn.: Greenwood Press, 1988).

RORTY, RICHARD, *Philosophy and the Mirror of Nature* (Oxford: Basil Blackwell, 1980).

—— *Consequences of Pragmatism: Essays 1972–1980* (Brighton: Harvester, 1982).

—— *Contingency, Irony and Solidarity* (Cambridge: Cambridge University Press, 1989).

ROWE, WILLIAM, *Philosophy of Religion: An Introduction* (Encino, Calif.: Dickenson Publishing Co., 1978).

RUNZO, JOSEPH, *Reason, Relativism and God* (Basingstoke: Macmillan, 1986).

SCHLEIERMACHER, FRIEDRICH, *On Religion, Addresses to its Cultured Critics*, trans. Terence N. Tice (Richmond, Va.: John Knox Press, 1909). (1821)

SURIN, KENNETH, *Theology and the Problem of Evil* (Oxford: Basil Blackwell, 1986).

SWINBURNE, RICHARD, *The Coherence of Theism* (Oxford: Clarendon Press, 1977).

—— *The Existence of God* (Oxford: Oxford University Press, 1979).

—— *Faith and Reason* (Oxford: Oxford University Press, 1981).

—— *The Evolution of the Soul* (Oxford: Clarendon Press, 1986).

SYKES, STEPHEN, *The Identity of Christianity* (London: SPCK, 1984).

TILLICH, PAUL, *Systematic Theology*, vol. ii (London: Nisbet and Co., 1953).

TILLICH, PAUL, 'The Two Types of Philosophy of Religion', in Paul Tillich, *Theology of Culture* (London: Oxford University Press, 1959).

TOMBERLIN, JAMES, and VAN INWAGEN, PETER (eds.), *Alvin Plantinga* (Dordrecht: Boston Publishing Co., 1985).

Troeltsch, Ernst, 'What Does "Essence of Christianity" Mean?', trans. Michael Pye, in Robert Morgan and Michael Pye (eds.), *Ernst Troeltsch: Writings on Theology and Religion* (London: Duckworth, 1977), 124–79. (1900)

VAN PEURSEN, C., *Ludwig Wittgenstein: An Introduction to his Philosophy*, trans. Rex Ambler (London: Faber and Faber, 1965).

WARD, KEITH, *The Concept of God* (Oxford: Basil Blackwell, 1974).

WEIL, SIMONE, *Waiting on God*, trans. Emma Craufurd (London: Routledge and Kegan Paul, 1951). (1950)

—— *Gravity and Grace*, trans. Emma Craufurd (London: Routledge and Kegan Paul, 1952). (1947)

WILLIAMS, BERNARD, 'Getting it Right', *London Review of Books* (23 Nov. 1989), 3.

WINCH, PETER, *The Idea of a Social Science* (London: Routledge and Kegan Paul, 1958).

—— 'Understanding a Primitive Society', *American Philosophical Quarterly*, i (1964), 307–24.

—— 'Language, Belief and Relativism', in H. D. Lewis (ed.), *Contemporary British Philosophy of Religion*, 4th edn. (London: George Allen and Unwin, 1976), 322–37.

WITTGENSTEIN, LUDWIG, *Tractatus Logico-Philosophicus*, trans. D. F. Pears and Brian McGuiness (London: Routledge and Kegan Paul, 1961). (1921)

—— 'A Lecture on Ethics', manuscript from notes taken by Friedrich Waismann, *Philosophical Review*, 74 (1965), 3–12. (1929 or 1930)

—— *Remarks on Colour*, trans. Linda McAlister and Margaret Schattle (Oxford: Basil Blackwell, 1951).

—— *Philosophical Investigations*, trans. G. E. M. Anscombe (Oxford: Basil Blackwell, 1953).

—— *Notebooks 1914–1916*, trans. G. E. M. Anscombe (Oxford: Basil Blackwell, 1961).

—— *Zettel*, trans. G. E. M. Anscombe (Oxford: Basil Blackwell, 1967).

—— *On Certainty*, trans. Dennis Paul and G. E. M. Anscombe (Oxford: Basil Blackwell, 1969).

—— *Lectures and Conversations on Aesthetics, Psychology and Religion*, compiled from notes taken by Yorick Smythies *et al.* (Oxford: Basil Blackwell, 1970).

—— 'Remarks on Frazer's Golden Bough', *The Human World*, No. 3 (May 1971), 18–41.

—— *Culture and Value*, trans. Peter Winch (Oxford: Basil Blackwell, 1980).

# INDEX

*Index*